Table of Contents

The Digital Heart

Mastering Emotional Intelligence in a Connected World

by

David Holman

Although the author and publisher have made every effort to ensure that the information in this book was correct at press time, the author and publisher do not assume and hereby disclaim any liability to any party for any loss, damage, or disruption caused by errors or omissions, whether such errors or omissions result from negligence, accident, or any other cause.

This publication is designed to provide accurate and authoritative information with regard to the subject matter covered. It is sold with the understanding that the publisher is not engaged in rendering professional services. If legal advice or other expert assistance is required, the services of a competent professional should be sought.

The fact that an organization or website is referred to in this work as a citation and/or a potential source of further information does not mean that the author or the publisher endorses the information the organization or website may provide or recommendations it may make.

Please remember that Internet websites listed in this work may have changed or disappeared between when this work was written and when it is read.

Contents

Introduction

In a world where our interactions are often mediated by screens and digital platforms, the nuances of emotional connection can easily be lost. Yet, in this same technologically-driven environment, the potential for enhancing our emotional intelligence is magnified. We live at the intersection of progress and emotion, where understanding and empathy are not merely add-ons but essential tools for navigating both our personal and professional landscapes. Emotional intelligence, once considered a soft skill, has become a critical factor for success and well-being in an increasingly digital world.

The digital age has gifted us with unprecedented opportunities to connect. We're capable of reaching across continents in seconds, collaborating with individuals from diverse backgrounds, and accessing an endless stream of information. However, these advancements also pose significant challenges. The anonymity and speed of online communication can often lead to misunderstandings, emotional misreads, and a decay in the quality of our connections. Here, emotional intelligence acts as a bridge, helping us to interpret, manage, and leverage emotions in digital interactions.

One might wonder, "What exactly is emotional intelligence in today's context?" It goes beyond the traditional understanding of recognizing and managing one's emotions and extends into the ability to navigate social complexities in virtual arenas. While the core principles remain, the application of emotional intelligence has shifted. It now encompasses reading emotional cues from text, empathizing through a video call, and managing one's emotional responses to the constant influx of digital stimulations.

The journey to mastering emotional intelligence starts with self-awareness. In the digital world, this involves understanding how our online presence affects others and recognizing our reactions to virtual interactions. It's about becoming cognizant of the small digital footprints we leave behind and the emotional repercussions they may have. By being aware, we lay the foundation for a deeper connection—not just with others but with our own emotions.

Embracing emotional intelligence online is not solely about managing negativity or conflict. It's also about building authentic relationships, fostering positive interactions, and ensuring our digital communications are reflective of our intentions. It's a skill set that meshes with every message we send, every post we like, and every email we craft. In effect, it's about infusing humanity into the virtual spaces we inhabit.

Our digital emotional intelligence is more crucial than ever in workplaces embracing remote operations. As teams span time zones and cultures, understanding the emotional undertones of communication transforms how we collaborate and lead. Emotional intelligence here is not just about efficient management; it's about creating environments where individuals feel seen and valued despite the physical distance.

Navigating this new frontier requires more than just an understanding of technology; it necessitates a keen insight into human behavior. The role of empathy cannot be overstated. When we interact online, we must strive to see beyond words on a screen. We must tune into the subtleties of virtual communication—the hesitations, the tone, the unspoken contexts. Empathy allows us to bridge the gap and foster genuine understanding, even without physical presence.

As we delve deeper into the nuances of digital emotional intelligence, we'll explore techniques to manage emotions effectively when screens become barriers. Whether it's taming the rising tide of online stress or crafting strategies for resolving digital disputes, the skills we build here will serve us not just in virtual spaces but enrich our real-world encounters as well.

Importantly, the goal is not to shun technology or retreat from our devices. Instead, it's about learning to use these tools in a way that enhances our emotional lives. Developing digital emotional intelligence empowers us to create meaningful connections that transcend the limitations of screens. It's about balance—ensuring our virtual lives don't eclipse our offline emotional health and finding harmony in how we engage with both worlds.

This exploration is both a personal and collective journey. Just as technology constantly evolves, so too must our emotional skills adapt. This adaptation is a lifelong endeavor, an ongoing process of learning and growing. Through this book, we aim to guide you in developing an emotional intelligence that not only meets the demands of today but anticipates the challenges of tomorrow. Whether through applications, future AI developments, or continuous learning, the path is one of growth.

In preparing to enhance your digital emotional intelligence, remember that change begins with awareness. It's about being open to new ideas, ready to adapt, and committed to a future where emotional intelligence is as digital as it is personal. Our world is rapidly changing, and by equipping ourselves with these skills, we not only keep pace but also create richer, more meaningful lives. Welcome to the journey of mastering emotional intelligence in the digital age.

Chapter 1: Understanding Emotional Intelligence

In today's hyper-connected world, emotional intelligence (EI) stands out as a critical skill set not just for personal growth but for professional success. It's fascinating how technology, while often accused of eroding face-to-face communication, can actually be an ally in enhancing our emotional skills. To understand EI in this era, we must grasp the fundamental attributes that form its foundation.

Emotional intelligence refers to the ability to recognize, understand, and manage our own emotions while also being able to identify and influence the emotions of others. In a digital age, these capabilities are often challenged by the lack of physical cues and the rapid pace of online interactions. Yet, the core components – self-awareness, self-regulation, motivation, empathy, and social skills – remain as relevant as ever. Mastering them can lead to more meaningful and productive digital engagements.

Embracing emotional intelligence isn't just about controlling emotions or avoiding conflict. It's about harnessing emotions as a source of energy and direction. Imagine being able to navigate an emotionally charged email without resorting to hasty replies that you later regret. Or envision the ability to empathize with a frustrated customer chatting from across the globe, transforming a potential grievance into a loyalty-building experience.

As we dive deeper into this book, you'll discover that developing emotional intelligence involves continuous practice and self-reflection. It's about implementing small, consistent changes that lead to lasting improvements in both online and offline relationships. The journey to enhancing your EI is full of rewarding insights and unexpected opportunities to connect more deeply with others.

Your journey begins by acknowledging how emotions influence every interaction, digital or otherwise. Once you recognize this, you'll be better equipped to navigate the digital landscape, making it a place of growth rather than of misunderstanding. Let's explore this essential competency and discover how it can redefine your personal and professional life.

Defining Emotional Intelligence in the Digital Age

Emotional intelligence (EI) in the digital age is an evolving concept that intersects with technology and human interaction. In essence, EI is our ability to perceive, control, and evaluate emotions, both in ourselves and in others. As we continue to integrate technology into nearly every facet of our lives, our emotional landscapes are shifting in ways that require a redefinition of EI to suit digital contexts.

In the past, EI focused primarily on in-person interactions. However, the rise of digital communication platforms—from emails and instant messaging to social media—has transformed the way we connect. These platforms introduce nuances that influence how emotions are expressed and perceived. For instance, in a text-based conversation, the absence of vocal tones and body language necessitates new skills in interpreting sentiments and intentions.

What does it mean to harness emotional intelligence in this digital realm? It involves adapting traditional EI skills to address the unique challenges posed by digital communications. This adaptation isn't just about transferring skills from offline to online; it's about evolving these skills to cater to the rapid pace and novel contexts of digital interactions. This means improving abilities such as reading digital body language, understanding the emotional undertones of written communication, and developing greater self-awareness about how our online personas may differ from who we are offline.

Fostering emotional intelligence in the digital age is not an optional skill; it's an imperative for personal and professional growth. Tech-savvy professionals may find themselves at the forefront of digital communication, often relying heavily on virtual interactions to conduct business or to maintain social ties. The effectiveness of these interactions is largely contingent on how well we can understand and manage our emotions, as well as empathize with others through virtual channels.

Consider how digital platforms allow for immediacy in communication. While this can foster quick connections and facilitate instant problem-solving, it also brings challenges. Without the visual or tonal clues to accompany words, misinterpretations can become commonplace. Thus, part of refining emotional intelligence in digital spaces involves developing a sensitivity to subtleties and consequently adjusting how we engage to ensure clarity and mutual understanding.

Empathy also finds new challenges and opportunities in the digital age. Conveying empathy through a screen lacks the instinctive nuances of face-to-face interactions. Yet, the digital arena provides unique opportunities to cultivate empathy across distances, cultures, and time zones—an advantage that wasn't possible a few decades ago. Developing digital empathy requires conscious effort to listen actively in online conversations, using language that shows understanding and compassion even in terse text exchanges.

Furthermore, the digital context makes self-awareness a key component of emotional intelligence. Our online behavior often reflects not just our current emotions, but also builds the digital narrative others perceive us by. Recognizing how emotions affect our digital footprint and choosing to present ourselves authentically, rather than reactively, is a crucial aspect of EI in the digital age.

Another dimension is the impact of anonymity and the 'online disinhibition effect,' where individuals may express themselves more freely, sometimes hurtfully, when shielded by the perceived distance and anonymity of digital platforms. Understanding this phenomenon is vital, as it can profoundly affect interactions, shaping not just individual communications but larger community dynamics as well.

As technology advances, so too must the strategies we employ to maintain and enhance our emotional intelligence. This evolution involves integrating new tools and methodologies, such as emotion-recognition technologies and AI-driven feedback, to better gauge and respond appropriately to emotional cues. However, the crux remains the same: to connect with others on a human level, fostering trust and mutual understanding across any medium.

In sum, defining emotional intelligence for the digital age is about more than just adapting our existing understanding of EI; it's about innovatively responding to the demands of a digitally interconnected world. By ensuring our emotional skills are as dynamic and adaptable as technology itself, we empower ourselves to build stronger, more meaningful relationships both online and offline.

Components of Emotional Intelligence

Emotional intelligence (EI) is a multifaceted construct that provides a framework for understanding and navigating one's emotions effectively. As we delve into the components that make up EI, it becomes evident how each plays a crucial role in enhancing our ability to connect with others, both online and offline. These components empower us to interpret our emotional responses and those of others, facilitating more meaningful interactions in today's digital world.

Self-awareness is the cornerstone of emotional intelligence. It involves an acute understanding of our emotions, what triggers them, and how they affect our thoughts and actions. Being self-aware enables us to monitor our emotions as they arise and adjust our behavior accordingly. In a digital context, this might mean understanding why a particular type of comment on social media evokes a strong emotional reaction in you. This awareness gives you the power to respond rather than react which is critical in maintaining your online presence with integrity.

Another essential component is **self-regulation.** Once you can identify your emotions, the next step is learning to manage them. This doesn't mean suppressing feelings or pretending they don't exist; rather, it's about channeling your emotions in a healthy, constructive manner. For tech-savvy individuals, this may translate to taking a few deep breaths before replying to an inflammatory email or deciding to disconnect from digital devices when feeling overwhelmed. Self-regulation helps in crafting a conscious lid on your impulses and is pivotal in sustaining professional decorum in virtual interactions.

Motivation, the drive that fuels goal achievement, is strongly tied to emotional intelligence. Intrinsic motivation is about being driven by internal rewards, such as a sense of accomplishment or the joy of creating something meaningful. In the tech world, this could mean pursuing innovative projects not just for monetary gain but for personal satisfaction and growth. Staying motivated in digital spaces is an emotional skill that ensures persistence in the face of challenges and technological disruptions.

The ability to **empathize** with others underpins our interactions and connections. Empathy involves understanding and sharing the feelings of others, an essential component in a world where more of our interactions occur through screens. It requires us to listen actively, interpret emotional cues, and respond with genuine care. In virtual teams, empathy can bridge the physical divide, fostering a sense of collegiality and understanding that enhances collaboration and creativity.

Social skills form the final pillar of emotional intelligence. These include the ability to manage relationships, communicate effectively, and influence others. In digital interactions, strong social skills mean knowing when and how to communicate, whether through emails, chat, or video calls, and adapting your communication style to the needs of your audience.

It's about crafting messages that resonate emotionally while maintaining clarity and professionalism regardless of the medium.

The interplay between these components of emotional intelligence is what truly enhances our interactions and relationships, particularly in the digital realm where personal connections are often mediated by technology. Developing EI allows us to bridge emotional gaps in virtual communications, leading to more effective collaborations and authentic relationships.

Enhancing these elements in oneself isn't just about individual growth; it's also about cultivating environments where others can thrive emotionally. By promoting emotional intelligence within professional settings, we create spaces where compassion, understanding, and innovation flourish. The impact of this is not limited to personal success; it contributes to a culture of empathy and resilience, vital traits in navigating the complexities of the modern world.

Further exploration of these components will reveal their interconnectedness and the remarkable ways they contribute to emotional and professional success. As digital environments continue to evolve, honing your emotional intelligence skills will be paramount in maintaining the balance between technological advancement and human connection. The journey into understanding and developing your emotional intelligence is not a solitary endeavor, but rather a comprehensive approach towards improving how we relate with ourselves and others in a rapidly changing digital landscape.

Chapter 2: Digital Communication Dynamics

The rise of digital communication has undeniably transformed our social landscape, weaving technology into the very fabric of our daily interactions. As we send texts and emails, participate in instant message chats, and engage in social media, we're often communicating in ways vastly different from traditional face-to-face encounters. This shift poses unique challenges and opportunities for developing our emotional intelligence (EI). In a digital world, understanding these dynamics is crucial for fostering genuine connections, as digital communication's nuanced complexities require a heightened awareness of emotional cues.

While technology offers unparalleled opportunities for connection, it also presents barriers that can impede authentic communication. The lack of physical presence often strip our interactions of vital non-verbal cues such as body language, tone, and facial expressions, which are pivotal in conveying emotions. In the absence of these cues, misunderstandings can easily arise, leading to misinterpretations that may strain relationships. Here lies the beauty and challenge: mastering the art of digital communication requires an amplified sense of empathy and attentiveness. By honing these skills, we empower ourselves to navigate this new realm of interaction with grace and effectiveness, enabling more profound connections.

Adapting to the rhythm of digital communication involves identifying and understanding context, intent, and emotion embedded within written words. This complex skill set demands a blend of patience and intuition; reading between the lines to grasp the unspoken elements of a message becomes essential. The ability to pause, consider, and truly digest digital content fosters not just better comprehension but also deepens the quality of our conversations and interactions. With every text and tweet, there lies an opportunity to practice and enhance our digital emotional intelligence, transforming potential obstacles into meaningful exchanges.

By embracing the dynamics of digital communication, we create a foundation for emotional intelligence that withstands the evolving tides of technology. This journey of exploration isn't just about adapting to new modes of interaction; it's also about fostering a deeper understanding of others and ourselves in the process. The principles of empathy, active listening, and thoughtful reflection remain relevant, bridging the gap between screens and souls.

The Impact of Digital Interactions

In the ever-evolving landscape of digital communication, the impact of digital interactions on emotional intelligence cannot be overstated. Our daily engagements are increasingly mediated by screens, transforming how we perceive and respond to the emotions of others. In a world where a single emoji can convey a multitude of sentiments, recognizing the nuances of digital communication becomes critical for maintaining meaningful connections.

Digital interactions present unique challenges and opportunities for enhancing our emotional intelligence. One standout advantage is accessibility; technology bridges geographical gaps, enabling us to connect with a diverse range of people from around the world. However, it also complicates the essence of traditional face-to-face interactions. The absence of vocal intonation and body language can lead to misunderstandings, and a seemingly benign text can drastically alter its meaning based on the recipient's interpretation.

The convenience of digital communication often encourages brevity, which can strip away the layers of emotion that would otherwise be present in a spoken conversation. When you're limited to 280 characters or less, how can you convey empathy, joy, or disappointment effectively? Sometimes, the fast-paced nature of online communication prioritizes efficiency over depth, but understanding this dynamic can lead us to new strategies for expressing emotions more effectively without sacrificing authenticity.

A critical element to consider is the permanence and public exposure inherent in digital discourse. Unlike fleeting conversations in the physical world, digital interactions can be archived, revisited, and shared, sometimes with unintended audiences. This can affect the authenticity with which individuals express themselves; the fear of judgement or backlash can lead to inauthentic interactions. Yet, this also positions digital platforms as powerful tools for introspection and reflection, offering a rich archive to analyze and refine one's emotional communication skills.

The anonymity afforded by digital communication equally adds a layer of complexity. On one hand, it can empower individuals to be more open and honest, particularly in expressing emotions or discussing traditionally stigmatized topics. On the other hand, the lack of accountability can foster negative behavior, such as cyberbullying, which can significantly impact emotional well-being. Navigating this duality is crucial for improving emotional intelligence in the digital age.

It's evident that digital interactions are shaping human connection, often blurring the lines between online and offline relationships. The virtual realm is not just an extension of our social lives but a significant domain where we learn, grow, and understand one another. Therefore, honing emotional intelligence in this context means acknowledging the transformative power of digital interactions while seeking to maintain emotional authenticity.

Understanding the impact of digital interactions on our personal and professional lives requires a balance between embracing technological advancements and preserving the core elements of human interaction. As virtual communication tools continue to embed themselves in every aspect of our lives, being mindful of their influence on our emotional landscapes becomes vital.

While the challenges are undeniable, digital interactions offer a profound opportunity to cultivate cross-cultural empathy. Engaging with diverse voices and experiences broadens our emotional understanding and enriches our perspectives, making us more adept at navigating complex emotional terrains. It is this opportunity that, if harnessed wisely, can be a powerful catalyst for personal growth.

Moreover, digital platforms have democratized the dissemination of emotional intelligence education. There is an abundance of online resources, communities, and courses aimed at developing emotional literacy. Individuals are no longer bound by geographical or socioeconomic barriers in accessing this knowledge, integrating it into their digital interactions to foster more supportive and understanding environments.

As we move forward in this interconnected digital landscape, it's crucial to foster environments that encourage genuine emotional connection. This involves creating spaces where individuals can freely express their emotions without fear of judgment, while also developing the resilience needed to engage with differing perspectives empathetically. The responsibility lies with both individuals and the creators of digital platforms to nurture an atmosphere that promotes healthy, constructive exchanges.

Ultimately, the impact of digital interactions on emotional intelligence is a multifaceted phenomenon that shapes our capabilities to connect, communicate, and coexist. Embracing the positives while mitigating the negatives can lead to enhanced emotional intelligence, bridging the gap between technology and humanity. As digital citizens, cultivating emotional awareness and adaptability in this context is not just beneficial—it's essential for thriving in our interconnected world.

Navigating Online Conversations

In the labyrinth of digital communication, the art of navigating online conversations is an essential skill for those looking to build meaningful connections. As technology reshapes how we interact, understanding the nuances of virtual communication becomes pivotal. Online spaces, from social media platforms to professional emails, offer both opportunities and challenges. This duality demands a refined level of emotional intelligence (EI) to interpret intentions, convey empathy, and maintain authenticity.

Online conversations strip away the context clues like facial expressions and tone of voice that are present in face-to-face interactions. This absence presents a unique challenge: the loss of non-verbal cues can lead to misinterpretations. It becomes crucial to enrich our written communications with emotional clarity. For example, consider using clear and concise language or emoticons appropriately to express tone, thereby strengthening the connection and facilitating understanding.

Digital spaces require us to hone our listening skills just as diligently as our speaking skills. Active listening online involves reading between the lines and asking clarifying questions rather than making assumptions. It's about knowing when to pause before responding, allowing you to process the information fully. This approach fosters thoughtful responses and deepens the interaction, creating an environment of mutual respect and understanding.

The way we manage our emotions during online conversations can significantly influence the outcome. It's easy to misinterpret a curt email or a brief text as rudeness or disinterest. Practicing patience and assuming positive intent are valuable strategies. Before reacting to something provocative, consider giving yourself a moment to reflect. Is there a possibility of misunderstanding? A simple re-read or query for more context can often reveal benign intentions. This mindfulness in interaction enhances both personal and professional relationships.

Crafting our digital persona thoughtfully is another crucial aspect of navigating online conversations. This includes being aware of the digital footprint you're creating with each post, comment, or message. Online, authenticity and consistency are key. Aligning your digital communication style with your real-world values will make your interactions feel genuine and relatable. This consistency builds trust and authenticity with others.

Empathy remains a cornerstone in any form of communication, and it's just as pertinent online. The digital divide, while vast, can be bridged by consciously incorporating empathy into our messages. Consider the perspectives and experiences of those on the receiving end. A simple acknowledgment of their situation or feelings can transform a transactional message into a compassionate dialogue. This practice nurtures a community of understanding and support within digital spaces.

Yet, online conversations also require boundaries. Engaging in every digital dialogue without limits can be exhausting and counterproductive. Set clear priorities about when and where to communicate, ensuring that online discussions don't intrude excessively into personal time and emotional space. This creates a balance that preserves your well-being while still being accessible and responsive in a professional context.

Technology also blesses us with tools that can enhance our communication. From grammar checks to emotional analysis software, leveraging these tools smartly can provide insights that improve how we express ourselves digitally. These aids can be particularly useful for those wanting to refine their tone or intention in their messages, helping align digital practices with emotional intelligence goals.

Additionally, managing the pace of online conversations is important. Instant messaging has set a high expectation for quick responses, which can fuel anxiety. It's perfectly acceptable—and often necessary—to set boundaries around response times. Letting your contacts know when you will be available for a conversation is a simple strategy that respects both your time and theirs, minimizing unnecessary pressure and stress.

Conflict, an inevitable aspect of any communication, takes on new dimensions online. Digital disagreements can escalate quickly without the moderating influence of face-to-face interaction. Employing emotional intelligence to de-escalate and resolve conflicts is crucial. This involves tactful word choices, a willingness to hear all sides, and a commitment to finding a mutually agreeable resolution. Such skills transform potentially divisive situations into opportunities for collaboration and growth.

In conclusion, navigating online conversations with emotional intelligence at the forefront is essential in today's digital age. It's not just about exchanging information but about building connections that enrich professional and personal lives. By understanding the dynamics of digital communication, embedding empathy, managing emotions wisely, and setting boundaries, we can communicate in ways that are both effective and emotionally satisfying.

Chapter 3: Building Digital Self-Awareness

In today's interconnected world, developing digital self-awareness is more than an optional skill—it's a necessity. As we navigate the myriad platforms and spaces online, understanding how we present ourselves and interact digitally can shape our relationships and influence perceptions. But what does it mean to be self-aware in a digital context? It involves a keen awareness of your online presence and the impact your digital footprints might have. This chapter explores that very journey, guiding you to become more conscious of yourself in the digital age.

Recognizing your online presence starts with introspection. Every profile photo, status update, or comment contributes to the digital narrative of who you are. Take a moment to reflect on what your digital persona conveys. Are you presenting an authentic version of yourself, or is there a disconnect between your online presence and real-world identity? By consistently examining this alignment, you bolster your digital self-awareness, making you more attuned to how others might perceive and engage with you.

Another vital aspect of digital self-awareness is monitoring your emotional triggers. The internet can be a minefield of emotional provocations, from heated discussions on social media to unexpected news alerts. It's essential to identify what sets off your emotional responses and why. Pay attention to moments when your reactions might overshadow your intentions. By recognizing these triggers, you empower yourself to respond with greater clarity and control, promoting healthier interactions online.

Building digital self-awareness isn't about curbing your digital expression but rather enhancing it through intentionality. As you grow more aware of the nuances of your online interactions, you cultivate a space that reflects your values and emotional intelligence. This purposeful approach not only uplifts your digital engagements but also enriches your offline interactions, creating a seamless blend between the virtual and the real world.

Recognizing Your Online Presence

In today's expansive digital realm, the concept of one's online presence is no longer confined to just a simple social media profile. It's an intricate blend of personal branding, digital footprints, and how you represent yourself across various online platforms. Recognizing your online presence is a crucial step in building digital self-awareness, a skill that tech-savvy individuals like yourself need to master to enhance emotional intelligence and interpersonal skills in this digital age.

Your online presence is essentially how you are perceived by others in the digital world. This includes everything from the photos and posts you share on social media to the comments you leave on blogs and forums. It's the collective representation of your digital activities and interactions. Recently, just having an account isn't enough. The nuance lies in understanding how these various facets contribute to how others see you. This awareness not only impacts your personal reputation but also influences your professional relationships and opportunities.

Have you ever taken a moment to search your name online? If not, this exercise can be both enlightening and instructive. The search results will provide a view into your online identity as perceived by others. It's an eye-opening way to gauge how you're coming across and to consider whether it aligns with the image you want to project. Remember, intention and perception don't always match. Developing digital self-awareness requires actively monitoring these perceptions and making conscious adjustments as needed.

But why does any of this matter, you might ask? For starters, personal and professional boundaries are blurring more than ever. Employers, clients, friends, and even acquaintances often form opinions about who you are based on your online footprint, sometimes even before meeting you in person. Your digital persona can often precede you, acting as a first impression. Whether it's your LinkedIn profile catching a potential employer's eye, or your tweet being discovered by a new collaborator, your digital content tells a story about who you are.

Building this self-awareness takes time and effort, but the benefits are manifold. Begin by evaluating the tone of your online interactions. Simply put, tone is everything in digital communication. Given the absence of body language and vocal tones online, the way we write holds significant weight. Are your posts and messages aligned with the way you intend to be perceived? Ensure your communication style reflects your personal and professional ethos.

Moreover, consider the content you choose to share with your online audience. Every post, photo, or comment becomes a piece of your digital narrative. Is your online presence reflecting the values and beliefs you cherish? Authenticity is key here. Your digital presence should naturally align with your true self, aspirations, and values. However, be mindful of how public or private you want this side of yourself to be. Regularly assess whether the content you share continues to truly reflect who you are or who you are becoming.

Another element to consider is the platforms you frequent and participate in. Each platform hosts a unique culture and community, and recognizing how your presence fits within these contexts is vital. For instance, the professional aura of LinkedIn will differ greatly from the friendly and informal nature of platforms like Instagram or Twitter. Tailoring your content and interactions to each platform can help maintain a consistent yet adaptable personal brand.

Monitoring your online presence doesn't have to be a burdensome task. In fact, there are numerous tools designed to help you manage and evaluate your digital footprint effectively. Google Alerts can notify you of mentions of your name online, while various social media management tools provide insights into how your posts are received. These tools are not just about vanity metrics; they offer critical insights into your digital interactions and reputation.

However, metrics and feedback are just the starting points. Beyond monitoring, take an active role in curating your digital environment. Engage with communities and discussions that enrich your understanding and align with your personal growth goals. The digital world is teeming with opportunities for learning and self-development. Be intentional about the spaces you decide to enter and the voices you choose to listen to.

Recognizing your online presence also means understanding the impact you have on others. In our interconnected world, every post has the potential to influence, inspire, or affect someone else. Be mindful of the ripple effect your online actions can create. This awareness fosters empathy, turning your digital presence into a force for good.

As you grow more conscious of your digital self, you'll find that this heightened awareness translates into improved emotional intelligence. You'll better understand the dynamics of online relationships and be more adept at navigating digital conversations. You'll become not just a participant in digital spaces but an active, thoughtful, and empathetic citizen of the online world.

To sum up, recognizing your online presence is an ongoing journey of self-discovery and adjustment. It's about owning the narrative of your digital identity and ensuring it matches up with the values and ambitions you hold dear. With each interaction, post, or comment, you have the chance to craft a digital footprint that authentically and positively represents who you are. As you continue on this journey of building digital self-awareness, remember that every step you take is a valuable investment in both your online persona and your offline relationships.

Monitoring Digital Emotional Triggers

In a world where digital interactions are as ubiquitous as breathing, self-awareness has evolved into an essential skill. It's imperative to realize that unlike face-to-face communications, the triggers that incite emotional reactions in digital spaces can be subtle and easily overlooked. This is precisely why monitoring emotional triggers online is crucial: it's about recognizing what spurs our feelings, both positive and negative, when we're behind a screen. By understanding these triggers, you can begin to cultivate a deeper digital self-awareness that extends beyond the screen and into real-world relationships.

Every interaction online leaves a breadcrumb trail of emotional triggers that affect us, even if we don't always realize it. For instance, a seemingly innocuous comment on a social media post might evoke a visceral emotional response. It can be as simple as an emoji or as complex as a deeply personal critique. Recognizing that the digital environment is teeming with such stimuli is the first step in managing how they impact our emotional well-being.

Start by identifying patterns. What kind of online content consistently makes you feel anxious, elated, or frustrated? Perhaps scrolling through your newsfeed before bed leaves you feeling restless, or maybe a particular topic on a forum never fails to push your buttons. By tuning into these patterns, you can begin to understand the emotional impact of your digital engagements. This awareness allows you to make conscious choices about the kind of content you consume and the interactions in which you engage.

One effective technique to monitor these triggers is to maintain a digital emotional journal. This isn't your average diary; it's a space dedicated to noting down the situations and emotions provoked by your online presence. When you recognize a spike in your feelings, pause for a moment and jot it down. What was the content? How did it make you feel? Over time, patterns will emerge, and you'll gain insight into what affects your mood positively or negatively.

Acknowledging these triggers is powerful, but acting upon them is transformative. Let's say you've identified that engaging in political debates online leaves you feeling drained and hostile. Understanding this, you might decide to set boundaries, perhaps by limiting your exposure to such discourse or scheduling these interactions when you're in a better headspace to handle them. The act of setting these boundaries is, in essence, an exercise in self-compassion and emotional regulation.

Emotions, once triggered, crave action. They want expression and resolution. Therefore, learning how to responsibly express these emotions in digital realms is key to maintaining your emotional health. Consider healthy outlets like discussing your feelings with a trusted friend online or participating in forums where emotional discourse is navigated with respect and understanding. The goal isn't to suppress emotions but to channel them constructively.

While emotional triggers can stem from specific incidents, they can also be deeply rooted in personal history and past experiences. This makes introspection an indispensable tool. Ask yourself whether certain triggers tap into unresolved issues or insecurities. For example, do posts about success and achievement cause agitation because they resonate with your own fears of inadequacy? Such insights not only deepen your understanding of self but prompt growth and healing.

Emotions in digital spaces are contagious. The collective mood of a chat room or comment section can influence your own state. Being aware of this emotional contagion is vital. Surround yourself with positive influences where possible. Curate your digital spaces carefully, and don't hesitate to mute or block sources that consistently generate negativity or discomfort. Prioritizing your emotional health over the fear of missing out can create a more nurturing online experience.

Technological advancements, such as algorithms, further complicate the landscape of digital triggers. They often curate content based on your past interactions, potentially reinforcing emotional stimuli. Being mindful of how algorithms shape your digital environment is part of building digital self-awareness. Taking control of these settings where possible, like adjusting privacy settings or content filters, empowers you to shape how digital spaces affect your emotions.

Importantly, digital triggers don't exist in isolation. They often interact with your offline realities, blending and amplifying your emotional experiences. Recognizing this interplay can help you anticipate and moderate your reactions. For instance, if you've had a tough day at work, be aware that you might be more susceptible to negative triggers online. Conversely, a supportive online interaction can uplift your offline mood significantly.

The journey to monitor and understand your digital emotional triggers is ongoing but invaluable. It requires consistent effort and reflection, as the digital landscape and its emotional stimuli are ever-evolving. As you become more adept at noticing and navigating these triggers, you'll find yourself more in tune with your emotions—not just in digital spaces, but in every aspect of your life. This enhanced self-awareness lays the foundation for healthier relationships, both online and offline, and fosters a more profound connection with your own emotional landscape.

Monitoring digital emotional triggers is a crucial component of building digital self-awareness, and it's an essential practice for anyone striving to develop emotional intelligence. The process of identifying, understanding, and adapting to these triggers leads to personal growth and a more balanced emotional life in an increasingly interconnected world.

Chapter 4: Managing Emotions in a Virtual World

In our increasingly digital world, managing emotions is more vital than ever. As our interactions shift into the virtual realm, understanding how to regulate our feelings online becomes a crucial skill. Digital environments can amplify emotions, making it easy to misinterpret messages, react impulsively, or feel overwhelmed. This chapter focuses on empowering you to navigate these challenges effectively and with grace.

One's emotional regulation toolkit begins with recognizing how digital spaces influence our emotional responses. Online interactions lack the nuances of face-to-face exchanges, often leading to misunderstandings and heightened stress. The anonymity and immediacy of the internet can also trigger stronger emotional reactions than we might experience offline. By acknowledging these dynamics, you can start to create strategies that help you remain centered despite the noise.

Techniques for managing emotions online are diverse and adaptable. For some, a simple pause before reacting to digital stimuli can make a world of difference. Taking deep breaths and embracing a moment of reflection allows us to respond more thoughtfully and less reactively. Others might find benefit in setting clear boundaries for technology use, such as designated offline times to decompress and recharge emotionally.

Digital stress is real, and it can be relentless. Building resilience involves not just avoidance but also proactive stress management strategies. Practicing mindfulness through short meditation sessions or engaging in digital detoxes periodically can help mitigate stress. Staying connected with supportive individuals, even virtually, provides a network for expressing and processing emotions healthily. Ultimately, the key to thriving in a virtual world is maintaining an awareness of our emotional states and adapting our strategies as needed.

By mastering these skills, you can not only manage your emotions more effectively but also enhance your online interactions, developing more meaningful connections and a stronger sense of digital well-being.

Techniques for Online Emotional Regulation

In today's interconnected world, emotions can be a complex web to navigate, especially when most of our interactions happen behind screens. While the virtual realm offers numerous advantages, it also presents distinct emotional challenges. The art of managing one's emotions online isn't just a skill but a necessity for maintaining personal and professional harmony. This involves recognizing how digital communication can trigger emotions and adopting strategies to manage them effectively.

It's essential to start by understanding what online emotional regulation entails. At its core, it's about being able to monitor and manage emotions while interacting digitally. Given that online communication often lacks contextual cues, such as tone and body language, individuals must be adept at recognizing the emotional undertones of messages and responses. By refining this skill, we can reduce misunderstandings and foster healthier relationships online.

One effective technique for emotional regulation is the practice of pause and reflect. When reading a message that triggers an emotional response, it's beneficial to take a step back before replying. A temporary pause provides time for reflection and prevents impulsive responses. Engaging in this habit encourages a more thoughtful and measured approach to digital communication, reducing the risk of escalation and conflict.

Another vital technique involves the use of positive self-talk, which can significantly influence how we regulate emotions online. Negative self-talk can amplify feelings of frustration, anger, or sadness, especially when misinterpreting digital messages. Replacing these negative affirmations with positive, affirming ones creates a mental buffer, helping to calm emotional responses and put communication into perspective.

Mindfulness is another powerful tool in the arsenal of online emotional regulation. Practicing mindfulness in digital interactions encourages awareness of one's emotional state and its impact on online behavior. This can involve being present and fully engaged during digital interactions, leading to more authentic exchanges. Techniques like deep breathing or brief moments of meditation before responding to digital stimuli can also foster a more mindful approach.

Utilizing journaling can be an excellent method for processing emotions related to digital interactions. By writing about online experiences and the emotions they evoke, individuals gain more insight into their emotional patterns. This reflection helps in identifying triggers and developing strategies for future interactions, promoting growth in emotional intelligence.

Moreover, setting clear digital boundaries is essential for emotional well-being. Defining when and how you're available online helps in managing emotional overload. Being constantly connected can be draining; thus, establishing specific times for digital interaction ensures a balanced approach, limiting emotional strain.

Incorporating empathy into online interactions also enhances emotional regulation. Reflecting on how others might feel in response to your messages can improve emotional exchanges. By considering different perspectives, we can tailor our communication in a way that is considerate and respectful, creating a more supportive digital environment.

It's also beneficial to utilize technology positively in managing emotions. Various apps and tools are designed to promote emotional well-being and can apply when navigating digital conversations. These might include emotion-tracking apps or meditation guides, which facilitate self-awareness and emotional insight.

Finally, seek feedback from trusted peers or mentors who understand the context of your digital interactions. Constructive feedback can highlight areas for improvement, providing external insights into your online emotional management strategies. This support system can be invaluable, offering perspectives that you might not have considered.

The journey of mastering online emotional regulation is ongoing, reflecting the dynamism of technology and human interaction. As we continue to engage with others in the virtual world, honing these techniques will empower us to maintain emotional stability, improve digital interactions, and enhance our overall emotional intelligence. The key is in embracing these tools with intention and an open mind, ever striving to bring a touch of human understanding to our digital lives.

Strategies for Handling Digital Stress

In today's digital world, the pace and volume of online interactions can be overwhelming. We've created environments where screens become our main conduit for communication, injecting unique challenges into the emotional landscape. Digital stress isn't just about information overload; it's an emotional response to the demands of digital spaces that constantly seek our attention. Understanding how to manage this stress is crucial for maintaining our well-being and relationships.

First, let's identify the stressors. Notifications ping relentlessly; emails pile up unchecked. There's that incessant need to stay updated or risk falling behind. But beyond this surface-level chaos, lies a deeper, more subconscious stressor: the emotional toll of perpetual connectivity. The expectation that we are always available can create an internal stress that gnaws away at our emotional resilience.

One of the most effective strategies to handle digital stress is to develop a digital mindfulness practice. This isn't about spending hours meditating in silence but finding moments of awareness amidst digital chaos. Begin with small, conscious decisions. Put the phone down during meals. Notice how often you check your email in an hour, and aim to reduce that number. Awareness precedes change, and by becoming conscious of our digital habits, we can begin to transform them.

A simple yet impactful technique is to set boundaries for digital consumption. It's about saying "no" to certain digital activities that don't serve your emotional health. Determine what times of day you'll check social media or turn off work emails. Apply the concept of "digital detox" without the pressure of quitting cold turkey. Reduce usage gradually. Establish tech-free zones in your home, like the bedroom or dining area. Boundaries aren't meant to restrict; they are tools to reclaim mental space.

In a world that lauds multitasking, the skill of single-tasking is underappreciated. Give yourself the gift of monotasking. Focus on one digital task at a time and do it fully. Whether it's responding to emails, participating in a video call, or simply enjoying a TV show, immerse yourself completely. This focus reduces the mental strain caused by juggling multiple digital streams.

Another key strategy is to engage in digital empathy. Realize that behind every screen is a human with emotions similar to yours. Lead with empathy in interactions. This not only alleviates stress for you but has a ripple effect on others. Being sensitive to the emotional undertones in digital messages, you become better equipped to respond appropriately, reducing the potential for miscommunication and conflict.

Further, it's important to curate your digital environment. We have more control than we realize over the kinds of content and interactions we engage with online. Take a moment to review your digital subscriptions, the people you follow, and the media you consume. Are they contributing positively to your emotional state or adding to the stress? Unfollow, mute, or unsubscribe from those that aren't serving your emotional needs.

The digital community can also be a source of support in managing stress. Use technology to connect meaningfully rather than superficially. Join groups or forums that align with your interests and values. These communities often offer emotional support that can buffer against the stressors of daily digital life.

Physical activity is another powerful antidote to digital stress. The irony is that even as technology connects us, it can lead to a sedentary lifestyle. Incorporate breaks throughout your day to move around and stretch. Physical movement not only benefits your body but clears mental fog and releases tension, making it easier to approach digital tasks with a fresh perspective.

When digital stress peaks, grounding techniques can be invaluable. Practice deep breathing exercises or the 5-4-3-2-1 sensory method, which can instantly bring you back to the present. These practices act as emotional anchors, pulling you out of stress spirals and back into balance.

Mindfulness practices are also instrumental in managing digital stress. Embrace activities like meditation or journaling, even if only for a few minutes a day. These practices calm the noise, allowing you to process emotions constructively instead of being reactive. By integrating mindfulness into your routine, speaking more consciously and reacting with intentionality become more effortless.

Finally, seek moments of digital solitude. Just as relationships thrive on quality time, so does your relationship with yourself. Schedule time away from screens to recharge. This isn't about disconnecting permanently but creating a balanced relationship with digital spaces so they don't eclipse your inner world.

In crafting these strategies, remember that changes take time. It's about small, consistent shifts that collectively foster an emotionally intelligent engagement with the digital realm. As we navigate this virtual world, let's prioritize emotional well-being and cultivate resilience. Empowered with these strategies, digital spaces can become sources of connection and growth, rather than stress.

Chapter 5: Developing Empathy in Digital Interactions

In an era dominated by screens and keyboards, empathy emerges as a crucial skill that bridges the communication gap. The digital world offers endless possibilities, but it also presents unique challenges for genuine connection. So, how do we cultivate empathy when the warmth of a human voice is often replaced by a blinking cursor?

The key lies in our ability to tune into the subtleties of online communication. Recognizing emotional cues hidden in text requires a heightened awareness of the words we choose and the tone they convey. As we type, we must consider the nuance and impact our words might have, even without vocal or visual cues. The challenge is to engage our imagination—to read between the lines and infer emotions that aren't explicitly stated.

Moreover, fostering empathy through screens demands a proactive effort to understand various perspectives. The digital landscape allows us to engage with diverse communities, offering an opportunity to broaden our understanding of different lifestyles and viewpoints. By consciously seeking out conversations with individuals from varied backgrounds and actively listening to their stories, we nurture our capacity for empathy.

Finally, empathy requires reflection. After interactions, taking a moment to ponder how your message was perceived can provide valuable insights. Did the recipient understand your intentions? Could you have expressed yourself differently to convey a sense of understanding and respect? Such reflection not only enhances personal growth but also strengthens the quality of future interactions.

Developing empathy in digital interactions isn't just a skill—it's an art. It transforms cold, impersonal exchanges into meaningful dialogues that resonate on a human level. Through empathy, we bring warmth and depth to our digital communications, crafting connections that defy the barriers of distance and screen.

Cultivating Empathy Through Screens

Cultivating empathy in digital interactions can feel like a daunting task, especially when human faces are reduced to pixels, and voices become text. Yet, empathy remains an essential skill in these interactions, as it forms the bridge that connects us, despite the distance. Empathy requires being present, truly understanding another person's feelings, and responding to them with care. In the digital space, where we often communicate through screens, this can be trickier, but not impossible. Our challenge is to overcome the abstraction of digital communication and reintroduce the human element into our interactions.

Let's consider how we communicate empathy through screens. Instead of relying on physical cues, we must become adept at recognizing and interpreting the subtler emotional cues embedded in written words, emojis, and even silences. For instance, a well-placed emoji can convey a wide range of emotions, from sympathy to enthusiasm, acting as a surrogate for tone and body language. Similarly, understanding the context and choice of words in text messages or emails can provide insights into the sender's emotional state.

Empathy through screens also demands that we listen actively, albeit digitally. This involves reading between the lines and pausing to truly digest what's being said before hastily crafting a response. One effective strategy is to reflect back what you've understood. Phrases like "It sounds like you're feeling..." or "I can see why that could be..." not only show that you're attentive but also invite further dialogue. This mirroring can validate feelings and foster a sense of connection, even across a screen.

Moreover, cultivating empathy requires self-awareness. Recognizing our inherent biases and how they might color our interpretations of digital communications is vital. Are we quick to assume an aggressive tone in an email because of past experiences? Practicing mindfulness can help us detach from these biases, allowing us to approach each digital interaction with an open mind.

To harness empathy, we must also acknowledge the limitations of digital interactions. Screens create a buffer that can desensitize us to the humanity of the person on the other side. To counter this, remind yourself that there's a real person with complex emotions behind every message. Over time, practicing this awareness can instinctively guide you to respond more empathetically.

Furthermore, empathy in digital interactions can be nourished by shared experiences and common interests. Topics that resonate personally can deepen connections and make the digital divide feel less daunting. By discussing shared passions or collaborating on projects, empathy and understanding naturally flourish, bridging the gap that screens can so often create.

As we develop empathy through screens, patience becomes a virtue. Miscommunications are inevitable, and not every emotional nuance will translate perfectly through digital mediums. When misunderstandings arise, patience allows for smoother reconciliation. It reminds us to take a step back, clarify rather than react defensively, and approach each situation with a growth mindset.

The practice of empathy is also intertwined with emotional resilience. We must be resilient to manage negative emotions effectively and maintain empathy in challenging interactions. Cultivating empathy involves learning from these encounters and growing stronger in our emotional intelligence.

Finally, empathy through screens is not confined to textual interactions. Video calls provide a richer tapestry of communication, where facial expressions and voice intonations become accessible. These visual and auditory cues can strengthen the bond that words alone may struggle to convey. While they come with their own set of challenges, video interactions offer an opportunity for a more conventional form of empathy, reminding us of the importance of retaining our humanity as technology evolves.

In conclusion, although screens introduce complexities in building empathy, they also present unique opportunities. By attentively listening, being self-aware, and showing patience, we can nurture empathy through our screens. With continuous practice and awareness, empathy can flourish in digital spaces, enhancing our relationships both online and offline. By making intentional efforts to understand and connect on a deeper level, we enrich our interactions and transform the digital landscape into a realm of empathy and connection.

Understanding Online Emotional Cues

In today's hyper-connected world, digital interactions are a significant part of our daily lives. While they bring convenience and speed, understanding emotional cues in this realm can be challenging. Yet, it's crucial for developing empathy in digital interactions, as interpreting someone's emotional state online often requires more than a mere glance at their words. Successful digital communication depends on our ability to read and respond to these subtle emotional signals accurately. As we become more adept at recognizing these cues, we also create pathways for deeper connections and more meaningful conversations.

One might think that the absence of facial expressions and tone of voice in online communication would hinder empathy, but that's not entirely the case. In fact, online platforms offer a unique set of emotional indicators if we know where to look. Emojis, punctuation, and even the timing of a message can all convey critical emotional context. An exclamation mark can signal enthusiasm or urgency; a carefully chosen emoji can soften the tone of a sentence or add levity. These elements are the modern counterparts to facial expressions and gestures, creating a new language of emotion that demands our attention.

It's essential to approach digital interactions with curiosity and awareness. Recognizing that each platform may have its own set of norms and emotional cues is integral to effectively reading and empathizing with others online. For example, a message that might come across as abrupt in an email could be perfectly acceptable in a quick text message exchange. This variation means that developing empathy requires flexibility and an adaptive mindset to navigate these diverse nuances successfully.

Context is another crucial factor. Understanding the emotional state of an online conversation often involves piecing together various elements, much like solving a puzzle. The context includes past interactions, the relationship dynamics between the individuals involved, and the specific circumstances surrounding the current exchange. It's only by combining these elements that you can fully appreciate the emotional undercurrent of a digital conversation and respond with genuine empathy.

One of the most effective tools for understanding online emotional cues is active listening or its digital equivalent, attentive reading. This involves focusing closely on the text, reading between the lines, and acknowledging the emotions that might be manifesting beyond the words. It's about becoming fully engaged with the content and resisting the urge to multitask while engaging in digital communication. Doing so demonstrates respect for the other person's input and builds trust and emotional connection.

Online communication can sometimes lead to misunderstandings due to the ambiguity of written words. Establishing clarity is vital for empathetic engagement. When in doubt, don't hesitate to ask for clarification. Questions like, "Can you tell me more about that?" or "How do you feel about this?" are not just tools for gaining understanding but also expressions of empathic interest. By inviting further dialogue, we allow for a shared emotional journey rather than making assumptions based on one-sided interpretations.

Empathy in digital interactions is also about being mindful of our emotional impact on others. The simplicity of typing words does not diminish their power. Hence, it's critical to consider the emotional consequences of our digital footprint. Taking a moment to review messages before sending them can prevent unintended emotional harm and reinforce positive communication dynamics. In the digital sphere, kindness and thoughtfulness are far-reaching. They transform ordinary interactions into opportunities for empathy and connection.

Furthermore, patience is a virtue that underpins our ability to understand emotional cues online. With the nature of digital communication often being asynchronous, it's important to give others time and space to articulate their thoughts and emotions. Responding thoughtfully, rather than impulsively, can result in exchanges that are more productive and emotionally satisfying.

The journey to mastering empathy in digital interactions involves continuous learning and reflection. By paying close attention to emotional cues, we can adapt our communication style to better meet the needs of the people we interact with. This personal adjustment not only fosters individual growth but also contributes to a more empathetic digital community at large.

In conclusion, understanding online emotional cues may seem challenging at first, but with practice and awareness, we can become skilled interpreters of digital emotions. As we hone these skills, we foster deeper, more meaningful connections that transcend the confines of screens and devices. By embracing this new emotional language, we not only enhance our online interactions but also enrich our real-world connections, ultimately leading to a more empathetic and understanding society.

Chapter 6: Strengthening Digital Relationships with Emotional Intelligence

In an era where digital interactions often take precedence over face-to-face communication, strengthening digital relationships through the lens of emotional intelligence has become essential. Emotional intelligence helps us not only understand our own emotions but also those of others, fostering an environment of mutual respect and understanding. By honing this skill set, we can transform our online exchanges into deeply meaningful connections.

The first step towards building trust in the digital realm is consistency. Showing up online as our genuine selves fosters reliability and transparency, cresting a foundation for trust. Utilizing emotional intelligence, we listen actively and empathetically, which confirms our interest in others' perspectives. We acknowledge their thoughts and emotions, demonstrating that they are valued and understood. This practice, simple yet profound, can significantly enhance online trust—a crucial element often sidelined in digital exchanges.

While technology can sometimes feel like a barrier, it also offers unique opportunities for cultivating meaningful relationships. Regular check-ins—even simple messages like "How have you been?"—can make a notable difference. These brief interactions signify that we care about others' well-being. With emotional intelligence as our guide, we respond thoughtfully, considering both words and subtext. Such awareness helps bridge the emotional gap that screens often create, weaving empathy into the digital fabric of our interactions.

Remember, meaningful digital interactions don't only revolve around big moments; they thrive on consistency and attentiveness. Acknowledging birthdays, celebrating achievements, or just sharing a laugh over a meme can nurture these connections. It's the little interactions, empowered by emotional intelligence, that enrich our virtual worlds and turn acquaintance into camaraderie.

Mastering the art of using emotional intelligence to strengthen our digital relationships isn't just good for others—it's beneficial for our well-being too. By creating and maintaining these connections, we bring a sense of community to our online lives, thus crafting a digital environment that is not just interactive but also deeply humane and fulfilling.

Building Trust in the Digital Sphere

In the vast expanse of the digital world, trust serves as the critical bridge linking us to others, whether they're long-time colleagues or new acquaintances. As our interactions shift increasingly online, this trust becomes both more essential and more challenging to establish. Given that we can't rely on the traditional cues of body language and vocal tone, we have to cultivate trust through other means. This calls for a heightened awareness of emotional intelligence, which plays a pivotal role in shaping and nurturing digital connections.

Crafting trust begins with authenticity. In digital spaces, authenticity isn't just about being honest; it's about presenting a consistent and genuine version of oneself across various platforms. When individuals perceive others as authentic, they're more likely to engage openly and reciprocate with their own authenticity. This creates a positive feedback loop that reinforces mutual trust. It's not just comforting to know someone's true intentions, but it's liberating for both parties involved. Through this authenticity, we lay a strong foundation for emotional connectivity.

However, the digital environment presents a unique set of challenges. The absence of face-to-face interaction can help create a sense of anonymity, which might lead some individuals to act differently than they would in person. This discrepancy often hinders the development of trust. To counter this, we need to adopt a mindset of transparency. Transparent communication—sharing intentions, thoughts, and even vulnerabilities—can demystify interactions and foster trust. In an era where skepticism and doubt can easily permeate online interactions, being upfront about desires, needs, and limitations can deter misunderstandings.

Moreover, trust-building extends beyond words. It's about recognizing and valuing the humanity that exists at the other end of the interaction, even if it's through a screen. When we acknowledge others' emotions and respond empathetically, we validate their experiences. This validation doesn't just aid in establishing trust; it nurtures it. By listening actively and responding thoughtfully, we bridge the emotional gaps that digital communication can sometimes create. This approach transforms transactional exchanges into meaningful relationships.

Empathy plays an influential role here. Understanding the feelings and perspectives of others, and showing that comprehension, is vital. In the digital sphere, people often face the misconception that empathic interactions are harder to achieve. But with careful attention to language and a commitment to listening—truly listening—empathy can flourish. For instance, using video calls instead of emails or messages can help capture visual cues and foster a deeper connection. Even small gestures like asking how someone is doing before diving into business matters can make a big difference.

The art of asking the right questions is another cornerstone in digital trust-building. Open-ended questions encourage dialogue and invite deeper insight, allowing people to express themselves authentically. By posing thoughtful questions, we show genuine interest in understanding the other person's perspectives and emotions, which in turn creates a safe space for them to share openly. This practice not only builds immediate trust but also contributes to long-term relational growth.

Additionally, consistency should not be overlooked. Whether it's timely responses to messages or maintaining the commitments made during interactions, consistency establishes reliability. When people know they can count on you, it subconsciously signals competence and integrity. In digital realms, where interactions sometimes lack the binding nature of physical contracts or agreements, demonstrating consistent behavior reinforces the notion that one's word holds weight, making it an integral part of trust-building.

Yet trust isn't a stagnant entity; it evolves. Regular check-ins, feedback loops, and open dialogues on how relationships are progressing can help assess and fortify trust continuously. When people feel like they're active participants in the evolution of the relationship, they're more likely to invest their trust and efforts earnestly. Digital tools and communication platforms can be leveraged to facilitate these ongoing conversations seamlessly, allowing relationships to grow sturdy amidst the dynamic backdrop of the digital age.

It's important to remember that breaches of trust can and do happen. In the digital realm, these breaches might be magnified due to the pervasive nature of digital communication. Therefore, cultivating a culture of accountability is essential. Owning up to mistakes and proactively working to rectify them demonstrates maturity and sincerity. This transparency can often transform breaches into opportunities for deeper understanding and stronger bonds.

Ultimately, building trust in the digital sphere isn't just an act—it's a continuous commitment. It's about weaving emotional intelligence into every thread of digital interaction. The ability to convey sincerity, demonstrate empathy, ask insightful questions, maintain consistency, and practice accountability are all vital elements in this complex yet rewarding endeavor. Through such practices, we don't just build trust; we become architects of meaningful and resilient digital relationships.

As we continue to navigate the ever-expanding digital world, let us harness the full potential of emotional intelligence. By doing so, we're not just creating connections; we're building trust that will withstand the test of time, transcending the limits of screens and devices, and reaching into the very heart of human interaction.

Maintaining Meaningful Connections Online

In an era where our fingertips can reach across the globe, it's remarkable how easily we can still feel disconnected. To maintain meaningful connections online, emotional intelligence isn't just an advantage—it's a necessity. As technology transforms the way we interact, the challenge lies not just in keeping in touch, but in genuinely connecting. While digital interactions can't replace the depth of face-to-face encounters, they can offer unique opportunities to strengthen relationships.

Understanding the emotional landscapes of our online communications starts with recognizing the limitations and possibilities of the medium. Digital platforms often strip away the non-verbal cues we lean on in physical conversations. Without facial expressions, vocal tones, or physical gestures, our words must work harder to convey empathy, understanding, and warmth. It's essential, therefore, to bolster our digital communication skills, intentionally focusing on the subtleties that might otherwise be lost.

Emotional intelligence in a digital context involves honing our skills of perspective-taking and active listening, albeit in written form. This might mean going the extra mile in reading between the lines, considering the emotion behind the text, and responding with thoughtfulness. One might think of it as turning up the volume on empathy. When we're mindful of our friends' and colleagues' feelings, we lay the groundwork for deeper connections that can flourish despite the screen.

Active compassion can also play a significant role in maintaining robust digital ties. Showing kindness and understanding in online interactions can fortify bonds that withstand time and distance. Whether it's a timely birthday wish or a thoughtful comment on a shared challenge, these small gestures are significant. They demonstrate an investment in the relationship and a willingness to be present, even in a digital space.

Creating communities and embracing digital rituals helps as well. Regular video calls with friends or group chats that celebrate daily successes can become cherished traditions. These rituals create a sense of belonging and continuity, anchoring relationships amidst the shifting sands of online communication. Communities form the backbone of online spaces where meaningful relationships can thrive. Participating in groups dedicated to interests or professional development can provide a sense of purpose and connection.

Attention to digital etiquette enhances our ability to maintain these connections. Simple acts like timely responses, respectful discourse, and acknowledging others' contributions to conversations reflect a high degree of emotional intelligence. It's about recognizing the people behind the avatars and treating every interaction with sincerity and respect. By doing so, we reinforce the human aspect of digital communication, fostering relationships that are not just transactional, but meaningful and lasting.

Moreover, tapping into the power of authenticity online is crucial. Sharing elements of our true selves helps build trust and rapport with others. While technology offers us a chance to curate our digital persona, it's the genuine moments—expressing vulnerabilities, sharing successes, admitting missteps—that resonate the most with others. Authenticity encourages reciprocity, leading to deeper, more meaningful exchanges.

However, maintaining meaningful connections isn't solely about what we project; it's about how we perceive and engage with others, too. Striving to understand different perspectives, valuing diversity in opinions, and practicing inclusive communication allow us to deeply connect with a variety of individuals. When we embrace the rich tapestry of human experience, it enriches our digital interactions and opens pathways to more profound connections.

Feedback and gratitude are vital components in strengthening online relationships. Offering thoughtful feedback can encourage growth and deepen mutual respect in personal and professional settings. Similarly, expressing gratitude—in messages, posts, or even emojis—creates a positive cycle of appreciation and acknowledgment. These expressions enhance emotional bonds and emphasize communal strength, leading to relationships that are supportive and enduring.

One can't overlook the challenges, though. Misinterpretation is a common pitfall in text-based communication, often due to the absence of tone and context. To counter this, clarity becomes paramount. Taking extra care in crafting our words, being explicit about our intentions, and asking for clarification when needed can prevent misunderstanding and reinforce trust.

Emotions can sometimes heighten in virtual spaces, leading to conflicts that, if not handled properly, can damage relationships. Here, emotional intelligence is our ally. By approaching digital disputes with empathy, patience, and a willingness to understand, we can de-escalate tensions and find common ground. It's about choosing to see beyond the immediate emotional reaction and focusing on the intention to bridge differences and maintain harmony.

As we continue to navigate the digital realm, embracing technology as a tool for emotional connection can transform our online relationships. Digital platforms can become spaces for collaboration, creativity, and community-building when used consciously and with intention. By continually adapting and applying emotional intelligence in our online communications, we're not just reacting to a changing world; we're actively shaping our digital interactions to be more fulfilling, resilient, and deeply connected.

In this journey of maintaining meaningful connections online, emotional intelligence is our compass. It guides us to understand others better, communicate more effectively, and nurture relationships that have the potential to enrich our lives. It's the key to turning a digital contact into a meaningful connection, ensuring that across the vast, boundless network of the digital age, we find a place of genuine connection.

Chapter 7: Conflict Resolution in Digital Spaces

In our hyper-connected world, digital conflicts are practically inevitable. Whether it's a misunderstanding in an email or a heated argument in a chat, resolving these tensions requires a new set of skills tailored for digital spaces. To navigate these waters effectively, one must first recognize the uniqueness of online interactions. The absence of tone and body language can amplify misunderstandings, making emotional intelligence crucial.

Start by identifying the root cause of the conflict. Often, what appears to be a disagreement is actually a miscommunication. Take a step back, breathe, and consider how emotions might be distorting perceptions. Approach the situation with a mindset of curiosity rather than judgment. Ask questions to understand the other person's perspective. This openness not only diffuses tension but also promotes a culture of empathy and understanding, fostering healthier interactions.

Active listening—a cornerstone of conflict resolution—needs a digital twist. In text-based mediums, where immediate feedback isn't always possible, ensure your responses reflect an understanding of the underlying emotional context. Summarize what you've understood before adding your viewpoint, demonstrating that you've genuinely engaged with their message. This practice can significantly reduce potential sparks in digital conversations.

Moreover, setting clear boundaries can help prevent conflicts from escalating. Declare what communication methods work best for you and encourage others to do the same. This transparency ensures that all parties are on the same page and know how to approach each other when tensions rise. By managing expectations, you create a digital environment that reduces the chances of conflict.

Finally, embrace technology as an ally in finding resolutions. Tools designed for collaboration not only streamline communication but also provide platforms for constructive dialogue. Whether using asynchronous message boards or real-time video calls, properly leveraging these tools can transform confrontations into bridges of understanding. By mastering emotional intelligence in digital spaces, you're not just resolving conflicts; you're paving the way for stronger, more compassionate connections.

Approaches to Online Disputes

In an era where our lives increasingly unfold online, understanding how to handle disputes in digital spaces is paramount. The anonymity and speed of online interactions can sometimes lead to misunderstandings and escalated conflicts. However, with the right approaches, it's possible to manage these disputes constructively and even turn them into opportunities for growth and connection.

Before diving into strategies for resolving online conflicts, it's vital to acknowledge why these disputes occur. Often, they stem from the lack of non-verbal cues that play such an integral role in face-to-face communications. Without gestures, tone of voice, or facial expressions, online messages can be easily misinterpreted. Additionally, the immediacy of digital platforms can encourage impulsive reactions. When tensions arise, the key is to pause before responding, thus allowing time to think and formulate a considerate response.

Adopting a mindset centered around empathy can significantly change the dynamics of online disputes. When someone feels misunderstood or attacked, their first reaction is often defensive. But approaching a disagreement with empathy involves trying to understand the other person's perspective. This doesn't mean you must agree with them; rather, it means recognizing their feelings and expressing that recognition. Phrases like "I see where you're coming from" or "I understand how that could have upset you" can help lower defenses and open pathways to productive dialogue.

In many cases, the medium of digital communication itself can influence how disputes are handled. Different platforms lend themselves to varied styles of communication. For example, a conflict on social media might benefit from a direct message rather than a public confrontation. Meanwhile, disputes that arise during video calls might necessitate verbal acknowledgment followed by a clarifying email, ensuring both immediate understanding and a documented follow-up.

A structured approach to conflict resolution can be invaluable. Start by clarifying the issue at hand. Often, what begins as a minor disagreement can spiral into a larger conflict when the original issue gets lost in emotional reactions. Clearly stating, "I think the core of our disagreement is..." helps center the conversation. Next, actively listen to the other party, making sure they feel heard. Active listening involves acknowledging their points, summarizing what has been said, and asking questions for further clarity.

Once the conversation is underway, maintain focus on the present dispute without dragging in past grievances. Keeping the conversation relevant and on point prevents it from becoming an unproductive airing of accumulated resentments. Strive for solutions that are collaborative and prioritize mutual understanding rather than simply 'winning' the argument.

Sometimes, despite best efforts, an online dispute may require external intervention. This might involve bringing in a neutral third party who can offer a fresh perspective and mediate the discussion. For business-related conflicts, seeking assistance from HR or professional mediators can be effective. Use of formal tools or platforms designed for conflict resolution, like mediation apps, can also contribute positively to handling disputes respectfully and efficiently.

Digital disputes aren't limited to one-on-one interactions. In group settings like forums or team chats, conflicts can involve multiple parties and viewpoints, making resolution more complex. Here, establishing ground rules for discussions and consistently enforcing them can prevent escalation. Encouraging all participants to take turns, respect each other's contributions, and avoid personal attacks fosters a respectful environment conducive to resolving disagreements.

Maintaining a solution-focused mindset is crucial. Once all parties have expressed their views and understood different perspectives, shift the focus to finding tangible, realistic solutions. This means brainstorming collaboratively to arrive at a resolution, or if necessary, agreeing to disagree while outlining steps to prevent future conflicts.

Investing effort into maintaining constructive relationships post-conflict can also transform digital disputes into growth opportunities. Reflect on what was learned from the disagreement and how it could inform future interactions. By resolving disputes amicably and learning from them, relationships can emerge stronger and more resilient, promoting a culture of open communication and mutual respect in digital spaces.

The evolving nature of our digital interactions means new challenges will continue to arise. But through developing emotional intelligence and a structured approach to handling disputes, individuals can enrich their online experiences and foster environments that reflect their best selves, both personally and professionally.

Techniques for Digital Negotiation

In our rapidly evolving digital landscape, the nature of negotiation has undergone significant transformations. As we navigate the shades of online interactions, digital negotiation emerges as an essential skill, requiring the careful application of emotional intelligence. Engaging in digital negotiation involves more than just exchanging information; it demands understanding, empathy, and strategic thinking. Let's delve into various techniques that can foster successful negotiation in these virtual corridors.

To begin with, recognizing tone in text is crucial. In the absence of vocal nuances and body language, the written word in digital communication can often bear ambiguity. Crafting messages with clarity and sensitivity ensures that the intent does not get lost. It's helpful to avoid jargon or any overly formal language which might create barriers. Similarly, reading your messages aloud before sending can give you a sense of how they might be received, reducing the risk of misinterpretation.

Active listening remains vital, even when communication is digital. This involves more than just passively reading emails or messages. It requires a conscious effort to grasp the underlying emotions and concerns of the other party. You can demonstrate digital active listening by acknowledging the other person's points thoughtfully, summarizing their key statements, and asking open-ended questions. The goal here is to make the other party feel heard and valued, thereby laying the groundwork for constructive dialogue.

Another key aspect of successful digital negotiation is the establishment of trust. Trust-building can appear daunting in virtual spaces because of the lack of immediate physical presence. However, consistency and reliability in your communications can bridge this gap. Respond promptly to messages, and maintain openness about intentions and mistakes. This transparency fosters a reputation for reliability, which can be pivotal in a negotiation setting.

Understanding cultural differences is becoming increasingly important as digital negotiations often occur across borders. What might be an accepted norm in one culture can be perceived differently in another. Educating yourself about the cultural backgrounds of your negotiation partners helps avoid misunderstandings. Customizing your approach to acknowledge and respect these differences doesn't just prevent conflicts but can enhance collaboration.

Managing emotions during negotiations is a technique that involves deliberate self-control and awareness. Digital spaces can sometimes create a sense of detachment that makes it easy to act impulsively. Practicing patience and restraint can prevent emotional flare-ups that may derail negotiations. If a message triggers a strong emotional reaction, it's often wise to step back, review your response, and take time before replying.

Moving negotiations from text to video calls can also play a significant role in digital spaces. Video calls retain some elements of face-to-face interactions, such as tone and facial expressions, which add layers of meaning to the conversation. They can help build rapport more effectively than text emails or messages. However, it's important to prepare for video negotiations by ensuring a stable internet connection and a distraction-free environment. This professionalism reflects your commitment to the negotiation process.

Framing your negotiation strategy involves setting clear goals and boundaries before you start. Knowing what you want from the negotiation, alongside the minimum acceptable outcome, gives you a roadmap that can be referred to throughout the process. It helps in maintaining focus and prevents emotions from dictating terms. Clear objectives also mean there's less chance for confusion, enhancing directness and understanding.

The use of technology and digital tools can also enhance negotiation techniques. There are several software solutions and apps available that can facilitate negotiations, track progress, and document agreements. These tools can help organize thoughts, keep track of correspondence, and remind negotiators of their goals, ensuring that nothing is overlooked.

Incorporating persuasive communication techniques into digital negotiation is another effective strategy. This involves using facts and logical arguments, aided by emotional appeals, to influence the other party. Tailoring your communication to highlight mutual benefits and align with the other person's values can pivot a negotiation to a positive resolution. However, persuasive tactics should be used ethically, as manipulation or deceit can damage long-term relationships.

Lastly, reflection is a crucial component of improving digital negotiation skills. After each negotiation, take time to reflect on what went well and what didn't. Analyzing these interactions can provide insights into how to enhance your approach for future negotiations. Reflection encourages learning from both successes and failures, continually refining your skills.

In conclusion, digital negotiation demands a finely-tuned balance of emotional intelligence, strategic communication, and careful use of technology. By embracing these techniques, tech-savvy individuals can navigate the complexities of digital negotiations with confidence and empathy, establishing and maintaining stronger, more productive online relationships.

Chapter 8: Balancing Digital Connectivity and Emotional Well-Being

In today's hyper-connected world, striking a balance between digital connectivity and emotional well-being has become more crucial than ever. While the digital realm offers endless possibilities for connection, information, and entertainment, it also poses significant challenges to our emotional health. It's vital to recognize that our digital habits can either foster emotional fulfillment or lead to an overwhelming sense of disconnection.

One of the key aspects of maintaining this balance is creating healthy digital boundaries. By setting limits on screen time and being mindful of the content we consume, we can protect our mental health and nurture real-world relationships. Adjusting notification settings, scheduling tech-free times, and being intentional about the apps and platforms we engage with are practical steps towards achieving harmony. These boundaries not only protect us from digital fatigue but also create space for reflection and emotional processing.

Equally important is prioritizing offline emotional fulfillment. While digital interactions can be convenient, they often lack the depth and nuance of in-person communication. Making time for face-to-face interactions with family and friends, engaging in physical activities, and pursuing hobbies can significantly enhance our emotional resilience. These activities anchor us in the present moment, encourage authentic connections, and allow us to recharge emotionally.

Balancing digital and emotional lives isn't about eliminating technology but integrating it thoughtfully into a well-rounded lifestyle. By investing in emotional intelligence, we empower ourselves to navigate the digital landscape with awareness and intention. This balance not only enriches our personal lives but also enhances our professional endeavors, enabling us to connect genuinely and empathetically with others in any setting.

Creating Healthy Digital Boundaries

In an era dominated by screens and instant connectivity, the lines between our digital and real lives often blur. This intersection can pose challenges to emotional well-being, making the creation of healthy digital boundaries imperative. With constant notifications, the allure of endless scrolling, and the pressing demands of virtual communication, it's easy to feel overwhelmed and emotionally drained. Establishing firm yet flexible boundaries can help us regain control and focus on maintaining a balanced emotional state.

Healthy digital boundaries don't mean closing yourself off from the online world; rather, they involve thoughtfully choosing how, when, and where you engage with it. This begins with self-awareness. Recognize the ways your digital interactions impact your emotions. For instance, consider how you feel after spending an extended period on social media. Are you uplifted, or do you find yourself comparing your life to others? Acknowledging these effects is the first step in crafting boundaries that support your emotional health.

Creating time-specific boundaries can also be beneficial. Designate certain hours of your day as technology-free. Perhaps mornings could be reserved for a screen-free routine, allowing you to start your day with intention and calm. Similarly, evenings away from the digital sphere can enhance your ability to unwind and promote better sleep. By consciously allocating time away from screens, you open up space for reflection, creativity, and authentic offline interactions.

Moreover, examining the quality of digital interactions is crucial. Engage in communications that are positive and meaningful, and try to steer clear of toxic interactions that sap your energy. This means selectively responding to messages that are beneficial and cutting down on unnecessary digital noise. Decide which notifications are essential and turn off the ones that aren't. It's about curating a digital environment that nurtures rather than depletes you.

Another vital aspect of setting digital boundaries involves being open and transparent with others about your digital availability. Communicate these boundaries with friends, family, and colleagues. Let them know when you won't be available to respond to messages immediately. This not only sets expectations but empowers others to create their boundaries as well. A culture of mutual respect for digital downtime can emerge when people are encouraged to prioritize emotional and mental health.

Balancing digital connectivity with emotional well-being isn't just about managing your own boundaries—it's also about respecting the boundaries of others. Be mindful of the expectations placed on digital communication. If someone doesn't respond right away, assume they are taking care of their personal need for space. This consideration fosters more empathetic and respectful digital interactions.

t's equally important to recognize when digital boundaries need to shift. Life circumstances change, and so should our boundaries. Be flexible and willing to adjust them as needed. Perhaps what once felt manageable is now overwhelming, or maybe you've acquired new insights into what enhances your well-being. Be proactive in revisiting and remodeling your boundaries to meet your current needs.

Incorporating periods of reflection into your routine can help you assess your digital habits. This might involve keeping a journal to track how time spent online makes you feel, or simply setting aside time for contemplation. Reflect on questions such as: "Are my current habits aligned with my well-being goals?" or "Do I have sufficient downtime to recharge?" These insights can guide the reevaluation and reinforcement of your digital boundaries.

Ultimately, the goal of establishing healthy digital boundaries is to cultivate a sense of balance and control over your emotional landscape. It's about empowering yourself to curate a digital presence that feels fulfilling rather than exhausting. When digital interactions are underpinned by intention and purpose, the result is a harmonious blend of connectivity and emotional well-being.

Embracing the challenge of creating digital boundaries is both an act of self-care and a strategic approach to nurturing emotional intelligence. As we navigate this digitally driven world, let's remind ourselves that it's not about disconnecting altogether. Instead, it's about connecting with the online world—and ourselves—in a way that enriches our lives. Recognizing the power we have to set boundaries can transform both our digital experience and our emotional health for the better.

Prioritizing Offline Emotional Fulfillment

In the midst of our hyper-connected world, it can be easy to feel like digital interactions are enough to sustain us emotionally. But, deep down, we know that the screen can only go so far. Real emotional fulfillment often requires offline interactions.

Human beings are wired for personal connections. It's part of our evolutionary makeup. The warmth of a smile, the sound of laughter, or even the comforting silence shared between friends can often mean more than a hundred text messages. While communicating online offers convenience and even a sense of community, it can't replace the richness of in-person bonds.

Crafting a balanced life that includes rich emotional offline engagement is vital. It requires intentionality; you need to decide that it's important and then take steps to make it happen. These face-to-face interactions provide the nuanced emotional feedback we miss in digital communication. They're crucial for our emotional health and well-being.

To prioritize offline emotional fulfillment, first evaluate your current life balance. Reflect on how much time you spend online compared to with people in real life. Are there activities you could swap out to make room for more face-to-face interactions? Perhaps that extra hour scrolling social media could be spent on a coffee date with a friend.

Building strong, in-person connections takes time and effort. Start small. Reach out to someone with whom you haven't spoken in a while. Arrange to meet in person. You might find that a simple conversation over a meal can rejuvenate your spirit like nothing else.

Creating offline bonds isn't only about friendship. It's also about building a network of support. Whether it's family, friends, coworkers, or community groups, each plays a unique role in our emotional ecosystem. Those offline moments amplify support, laughter, and warmth, giving us a foundation that holds steady when life becomes demanding.

How do we make this shift? Begin by setting clear distinctions between your online and offline life. Dedicate time to unplug completely, and use it for activities that nurture your emotional well-being. Spending time in nature, exercising, or pursuing a hobby can be revitalizing.

Remember the power of rituals and traditions. They provide structure and help forge emotional bonds. Whether it's a weekly family dinner, a monthly book club, or a Sunday afternoon hike, these regular activities create enduring emotional connections.

Emphasize quality over quantity. A meaningful 30-minute conversation with a loved one, free of distractions, can have more impact than hours spent on superficial chats online. Deep and engaging conversations help us feel heard and understood, which is crucial for emotional growth.

Consider how you can integrate these practices into your work life as well. The concepts of balance apply here too. Try holding meetings outside the office when possible, add more face-to-face discussions rather than email chains, and make time for genuine connection with your co-workers.

For tech-savvy individuals, it's often helpful to use technology to your advantage in prioritizing offline emotional fulfillment. Set reminders to step away from the screen, schedule regular downtime, and use digital tools to manage your time effectively so you can maximize face-to-face engagements.

In our pursuit of offline emotional fulfillment, let's not forget the importance of presence. Be present in the moments you create. It's tempting to check your phone during those face-to-face interactions, but avoiding this habit will significantly enrich your experience. Active listening and genuine engagement are gifts you give to both yourself and the other person in the conversation.

Finally, don't underestimate the importance of self-reflection to understand what truly fulfills you emotionally. Meditation, journaling, or simply taking some time to ponder can offer insights into what you value in your offline relationships. Knowing this can guide your efforts to achieve more profound emotional satisfaction.

The journey to achieving offline emotional fulfillment is both personal and profound. It might require stepping out of your comfort zone, but the rewards are innumerable. The face-to-face connections you nurture today become the friendships, support systems, and memories you cherish tomorrow. Activities, where emotions ride on a wave of genuine human interaction, have the power to transform your emotional landscape and enrich your life in ways a digital connection simply cannot.

Chapter 9: Emotional Intelligence for Remote Work and Virtual Teams

Remote work and virtual teams have rapidly become the norm, transforming how we connect, collaborate, and communicate. This evolution also presents unique challenges, particularly in terms of maintaining strong interpersonal relationships. Emotional intelligence plays a crucial role in navigating these challenges by enhancing team dynamics through understanding, empathy, and quick adaptation to digital environments.

The heart of emotional intelligence in remote work is the ability to empathize across screens. A high level of emotional awareness allows professionals to perceive the unspoken cues in emails, video calls, or chat messages. This skill is vital, as emotional cues are often less apparent in digital communication. Team members who are adept at recognizing these subtleties can anticipate misunderstandings, address frustrations early, and build a more cohesive team atmosphere.

Leaders in virtual settings face additional hurdles, as they must inspire and motivate teams without the benefit of physical presence. Emotional intelligence in such roles involves not just understanding team members' feelings but also effectively conveying one's own. Digital leaders who practice openness, active listening, and transparent communication can create inclusive environments that foster trust and motivation.

Moreover, emotional intelligence helps individuals handle the stress and isolation often associated with remote work. Implementing emotional self-care practices like mindfulness and emotional regulation techniques can mitigate the impact of such stressors. By maintaining their emotional well-being, professionals are better equipped to contribute positively to their teams.

Ultimately, emotional intelligence is the bridge that transforms remote work from a transactional interaction into a collaborative experience. It enables teams to move beyond basic communication, encouraging innovation and resilience. Harnessing emotional skills in a virtual context not only enhances individual performance but also leads to more successful, fulfilling team dynamics.

Enhancing Team Dynamics with Emotional Skills

In the era of remote work, the dynamics within virtual teams have become increasingly complex. While technology enables us to connect efficiently across the globe, the absence of physical interaction presents unique challenges that require emotional intelligence to navigate successfully. It's no longer enough just to be familiar with digital tools and platforms; understanding and managing emotions in yourself and others becomes a critical factor in fostering effective team dynamics.

One of the key components of enhancing team dynamics is active awareness of emotional cues. In a physical setting, body language and facial expressions offer rich information. Online, these cues are largely absent. This requires team members to hone their listening skills and pay closer attention to tone, phrasing, and even silence. Understanding that a curt email might signal the sender's stress or frustration, and not necessarily rudeness, is a skill that elevates the emotional intelligence of any team.

An important aspect is developing empathy within the team. Empathy allows team members to put themselves in each other's shoes, facilitating understanding and cooperation. This doesn't mean everyone needs to agree all the time, but creating a culture where everyone feels heard and valued is crucial. Encouraging team members to share more about themselves—like starting meetings with personal check-ins or casual conversations—can build deeper connections.

Building trust is foundational to any team dynamic, but it's even more critical in virtual environments. Without the daily in-person interactions to foster rapport, teams must work intentionally to cultivate trust. This can be achieved through transparent communication, reliability, and accountability. When team members consistently follow through on their commitments, it strengthens trust, paving the way for a more cohesive team.

Managing conflicts digitally requires as much, if not more, emotional intelligence. Online disagreements can escalate quickly if not handled with care. Team members should be encouraged to address issues directly rather than letting them fester. This involves approaching conflicts with a mindset geared towards resolution, focusing on the problem rather than personal attacks, and utilizing digital tools that facilitate constructive communication, like video calls over text-based messages.

Leaders have a substantial role in enhancing team dynamics by fostering an environment of psychological safety. They should encourage openness and vulnerability, allowing team members to express their views without fear of negative consequences. This involves acknowledging mistakes and learning from them, not punishing them, which can bolster innovation and creativity within the team.

It's also essential for leaders to recognize and celebrate achievements, big and small. Celebrating wins, whether it's a project completion or someone's birthday, reinforces team spirit. Using digital platforms to spotlight achievements can keep team morale high and remind everyone that their contributions matter.

Moreover, balancing the need for connection with autonomy is crucial. Virtual teams benefit from regular touchpoints, but excessive meetings can lead to burnout. Leaders should empower team members by trusting them to work independently while providing the support needed to succeed. Offering flexibility not only respects individual working styles but also nurtures a sense of belonging and commitment to the team's goals.

Ultimately, enhancing team dynamics in virtual settings is about fostering an environment where each member feels understood, valued, and part of something larger than themselves. When teams operate with high emotional intelligence, they are not only more efficient but also more resilient, navigating the complexities of remote work with agility and grace. As technology continues to evolve, the ability to harness emotional skills will remain a crucial differentiator for successful teams in the digital age.

Navigating Digital Leadership Challenges

In today's rapidly evolving digital world, leadership has taken on new dimensions, stretching beyond traditional face-to-face interactions to encompass virtual and remote environments. As leaders manage teams scattered across different geographies, mastering emotional intelligence becomes crucial. The digital leader of today must navigate not only the technical aspects of virtual work but also the subtleties of human connection through a screen. This chapter delves into the unique challenges and opportunities presented by digital leadership, highlighting the pivotal role emotional intelligence plays in steering teams toward success.

Effective digital leadership begins with self-awareness. Leaders need to be conscious of their own emotional landscape, especially when operating in a digital space where clues from body language and facial expressions are limited or absent. Understanding one's emotional state allows a leader to communicate more clearly and authentically, setting a tone of openness and trust. It's essential for a leader to recognize the impact of their digital presence on the team, assessing whether their virtual interactions engage and inspire or inadvertently create distance.

Communication is the lifeblood of effective leadership, and in virtual settings, it demands even greater attention. Leaders must cultivate the ability to read between the lines of text-based messages and to discern emotional cues from video calls. This requires honing an acute sensitivity to tone and context, acknowledging that digital mediums can easily amplify misunderstandings. Empathy plays a vital role here—leaders must actively engage with their teams' perspectives and concerns, addressing issues with compassion and understanding.

A particular challenge in digital leadership is fostering a sense of belonging and cohesion in a dispersed team. Without the physical comradery of an office environment, leaders must be creative in building team spirit. Virtual team-building activities, regular check-ins, and encouraging informal interactions can help strengthen bonds. Additionally, leaders should prioritize inclusive practices, ensuring that all team members feel valued and heard, regardless of their physical location.

Another hurdle digital leaders face is managing conflict within the team. Conflicts can quickly escalate in a virtual environment where messages lack the nuances of face-to-face communication. Leaders must be adept at identifying brewing tensions, often discernible from subtle changes in communication patterns or engagement levels. Proactively addressing conflict with transparent and direct dialogue prevents escalation and reinforces a culture of mutual respect and understanding.

Trust is the cornerstone of any successful team, and fostering it requires deliberate effort in a digital setting. Leaders must demonstrate consistency and integrity in their actions and words. By meeting commitments and being transparent about challenges and decisions, leaders cultivate an atmosphere of reliability. Encouraging team members to take ownership of their work and acknowledging their achievements also fosters trust, empowering individuals and enhancing collective accountability.

Leadership in the digital age also involves guiding teams through technological change. As new tools and platforms emerge, leaders must be adaptable and forward-thinking, ready to embrace changes that can drive productivity and collaboration. Equipping the team with the necessary skills and a mindset open to innovation ensures that technological advancements become opportunities rather than obstacles.

Moreover, digital leaders must be champions of work-life balance, advocating for healthy boundaries between online responsibilities and personal time. Encouraging team members to disconnect after work hours and respect each other's downtime preserves well-being and prevents burnout. Leading by example, a leader should model these boundaries, demonstrating their commitment to work-life harmony.

Acknowledging the diverse backgrounds and experiences of team members, particularly in a global context, is another critical aspect of digital leadership. Leaders should strive to create an inclusive culture by inviting diverse perspectives and leveraging the unique strengths of each team member. Promoting cross-cultural understanding and collaboration can enhance creativity and innovation, turning diversity into a powerful asset.

In essence, navigating digital leadership challenges demands a nuanced blend of emotional intelligence, empathy, and proactive communication. By prioritizing emotional connection and fostering an inclusive and adaptable team culture, leaders can transform the challenges of digital environments into opportunities for growth and success. As emotional intelligence continues to shape the landscape of digital leadership, those who embrace it will inspire teams that are cohesive, motivated, and resilient, ready to thrive in the face of change.

Chapter 10: Social Media and Emotional Intelligence

Social media, while an incredible tool for connection, also presents unique challenges for emotional intelligence. It's a space where emotions can run high and unchecked, often leading to misunderstandings or conflicts. Understanding emotional responses triggered by social media interactions becomes crucial. It's all too easy to react impulsively, missing the pause that allows us to respond with clarity and understanding. Recognizing these reactions and managing them fosters more authentic connections and helps maintain emotional balance.

On social platforms, where many present curated versions of their lives, the line between authenticity and facade often blurs. Striking a balance between being genuine and maintaining privacy can be tricky. By staying true to our values and communicating honestly, we encourage others to do the same, enhancing mutual trust and understanding. Authenticity isn't just about what we share but also how we respond to others. It's about being present, listening actively, and resisting the urge to perform.

Moreover, emotional intelligence involves understanding the impact of our digital footprint. Every comment, like, or share contributes to a narrative of who we are online. Mindfulness in these interactions promotes environments of respect and empathy. Whether it's a thoughtful comment or showing support through a simple like, our actions can be powerful tools for positive emotional exchanges.

For many, social media is an integral part of daily life, yet its dynamics can affect emotional well-being. It's vital to set boundaries to prevent emotional exhaustion. This may involve limiting screen time or curating a feed that supports positivity and growth. By prioritizing emotional intelligence in our digital interactions, we not only improve our own well-being but also contribute to healthier online communities.

Enhancing emotional intelligence in social media use isn't just about reducing conflict—it's about enriching our online experiences with deeper understanding and genuine connections. As we continue to integrate digital interactions into our lives, maintaining a mindful approach to social media becomes essential. Through intentional engagement, we can transform how we relate to others across the digital landscape.

Managing Emotional Responses on Social Platforms

The pervasive spread of social media into our daily lives means that we're often just a few clicks away from experiencing a potent mix of emotions. Social platforms, with their continuous stream of posts, comments, and reactions, can evoke feelings ranging from joy and excitement to anger and sadness. It's crucial, then, to build a toolkit for managing these emotional responses effectively, enhancing one's emotional intelligence in the process.

First, understanding the source of your emotional responses is essential. Social media platforms are designed to be engaging, often triggering instant reactions that might not reflect our true feelings. Consider how a single post or comment can rapidly alter your mood. This immediacy often leaves little room for reflection, leading to impulsive interactions. Being aware of the stimuli that provoke these emotional shifts is the initial step towards managing them. A sudden feeling of jealousy over a friend's vacation photos, for instance, could signal underlying insecurities about one's own lifestyle.

One effective strategy is to create a moment of pause before responding to content that stirs strong emotions. This pause, even if just a few seconds, allows reflection and a measured response rather than a knee-jerk reaction. It's akin to taking a deep breath during a heated offline conversation. Practicing this pause helps in maintaining control and responding with intention rather than impulsivity.

Understanding intent and context is also vital. Text-based communications lack the nuance of vocal tone and body language, leaving them open to misinterpretation. A humorous comment might be perceived as an insult, or constructive criticism might feel like an attack. By considering the context and intent, we can better manage our emotional responses and choose whether and how to engage or disengage.

Self-awareness plays a significant role in this process. Recognizing your emotional triggers on social media can prevent emotionally charged interactions. Reflect on past experiences: What type of content typically elicits strong reactions from you? Is it political discourse, lifestyle comparisons, or perhaps discussions on sensitive topics? By identifying these triggers, you can prepare yourself to engage with or avoid certain content, mitigating unnecessary emotional stress.

Additionally, it can be beneficial to curate your social media environment actively. Social platforms offer tools to mute, unfollow, or block content that consistently evokes negative emotions. By shaping your digital sphere to support your well-being, you can focus on content that aligns with your values and contributes positively to your life. Remember, it's your digital space, and maintaining a healthy environment within it is your right.

Reflective writing or journaling about your social media experiences can also enhance emotional regulation. Writing down thoughts and feelings related to particular social interactions helps to articulate unspoken emotions, offering insights into recurring patterns of behavior and response. This awareness fosters growth and equips individuals to handle future similar encounters with greater emotional resilience.

For those deeply affected by social comparisons, gratitude practices can be transformative. Regularly acknowledging and documenting things you're thankful for can shift your focus from what others have to what you already possess. This shift not only reduces envy but also enhances overall emotional well-being, reaffirming self-worth and contentment.

In moments of heightened emotional response, seeking support from trusted friends or mentors can provide perspective. Sometimes, an external viewpoint can highlight biases or assumptions you might have overlooked in your emotional state. Sharing your experiences and discussing them with others can help dissolve intense feelings and promote clearer understanding.

Engaging in mindfulness exercises tailors one's capacity to remain present and grounded amidst the emotional turbulence of social media. Mindfulness emphasizes living in the moment and fully experiencing emotions without judgment. Practices such as deep-breathing exercises or guided meditations can serve as anchors in moments of digital distress, calming the mind and allowing for purposeful reactions.

It's also essential to acknowledge the positive potentials of social media in emotional growth. Engaging with diverse viewpoints, finding supportive communities, and sharing personal narratives can lead to enhanced empathy and social understanding. Recognize the benefits that compassionate listening and open-mindedness can bring, not just to personal growth but to the broader digital community.

In summary, managing emotional responses on social platforms is a critical aspect of developing emotional intelligence in today's digital age. It involves a conscious effort to pause, reflect, and respond intentionally. By embracing these practices, individuals can navigate social media with greater resilience, fostering healthier and more fulfilling interactions both online and offline.

Ensuring Authenticity in Online Interactions

Authenticity in online interactions is more than just a buzzword; it's a core component of emotional intelligence in the digital age. In a world where communication happens behind screens, the challenge is to ensure that our virtual selves reflect our true selves. Achieving this is not only about being genuine but also about creating connections that resonate with sincerity and depth. When we approach our online interactions with clarity and honesty, we open a pathway to building trust and meaningful relationships.

At its heart, authenticity online begins with self-awareness. Recognizing who we are and what we genuinely value lays the foundation. Rather than constructing a digital persona based on how we wish to be perceived, we flourish when we allow our true selves to shine through. This doesn't mean we broadcast every emotion or detail of our lives; it's about consistency and coherence between our inner beliefs and outward expressions.

The digital environment offers anonymity and distance, often tempting us to present a polished version of ourselves. Platforms like social media, where likes and shares are the currency, can encourage performative behavior. Yet, the paradox here is that while curated personas may seem appealing, they rarely contribute to genuine connections. People resonate with experiences and emotions that feel real, and they can often spot a facade from miles away.

Consider your social media presence. Do the stories and images you share reflect the full spectrum of your experiences? Making a conscious effort to post content that is true to your values can act as a grounding practice. There's no obligation to share everything, but when you do, let it be with intention and honesty. Your narrative should be yours to tell, devoid of undue influence from external validation.

An effective approach to maintaining authenticity is balancing vulnerability with privacy. While vulnerability can invite connections and sympathy, it's crucial to guard your boundaries. Emotional intelligence equips us to discern what to share and when. Knowing where to draw the line is not about hiding; it's about preserving the integrity of your private world.

Moreover, understanding the impact of your online persona on others underscores the importance of authenticity. Our words and actions in digital spaces contribute to the collective emotional climate. From professional environments to personal interactions, authenticity fosters trust, creating spaces where empathy and understanding thrive. Such environments are fertile grounds for innovation, collaboration, and support.

Emotional cues, such as tone and body language, are absent in online messages, making the intention behind words paramount. Intentional communication that reflects our true sentiments helps compensate for this absence. Choosing words that align with your emotional state and conveying them unequivocally diminishes misunderstandings and misinterpretations.

To ensure authenticity, it's vital to engage with others thoughtfully. Pause before responding, especially in emotionally charged situations. This allows time for reflection, ensuring that your replies embody truth and not just immediate reactions. Thoughtful communication requires effort but pays dividends in the form of relationships built on understanding and respect.

It's also worth noting the role of active listening, even in textual forms of communication. Just as in face-to-face interactions, taking the time to truly "listen" to what others are expressing online makes a substantial difference. Practice reading with the intent to understand rather than merely to respond. This deepens empathy and reinforces connections.

In virtual interactions, personal growth and authenticity go hand in hand. Challenges faced online can prompt introspection and adaptation. Strive to integrate lessons learned from digital exchanges into your daily life, constantly refining your emotional intelligence. This enables a harmony between your digital and physical selves, reducing any disconnect between the two worlds.

Let's not forget the communal aspect of online spaces. Whether in forums, social media groups, or professional networks, these platforms thrive when individuals contribute authentically. Sharing genuine experiences and insights enriches the collective knowledge base, inspiring others to do the same. This ripple effect nurtures a culture of transparency and authenticity.

Ultimately, ensuring authenticity in online interactions is a continual journey of aligning your digital life with your true self. It's about maintaining consistency in your actions and interactions, fostering trust, and creating spaces where genuine emotional connections can flourish. As you navigate the digital landscapes, embrace the opportunity to express and enhance your emotional intelligence. It's a choice that leads to richer, more meaningful connections and a deeper understanding of both yourself and others.

Chapter 11: Technology's Role in Personal Emotional Development

In our modern world, technology is more than just a tool; it's a critical player in shaping our emotional landscapes. As we integrate digital devices into almost every aspect of our lives, they increasingly influence how we perceive and process emotions. Technology provides us with unprecedented access to resources and communities, offering pathways to develop emotional intelligence in ways that weren't imaginable a few decades ago. It's crucial, however, to consciously harness these digital advances for personal growth rather than letting them dictate our emotional responses.

Apps and online platforms designed specifically for emotional development have opened up new avenues for self-discovery. Whether it's meditation, therapy, or self-reflection, these tools can guide users toward greater emotional awareness and resilience. They serve as virtual companions, offering personalized feedback and reminders to practice mindfulness or gratitude. Yet, with this powerful convenience comes responsibility. Users must be intentional about their interaction with these tools, ensuring they complement rather than replace genuine human connections and self-exploration.

Looking ahead, artificial intelligence holds significant potential for further transforming our approach to emotional intelligence. AI-driven systems can analyze emotional responses, providing insights into patterns and triggers. However, the ethical considerations surrounding privacy and dependency must be addressed. The goal should be to empower individuals, not to route them through a one-size-fits-all solution.

By embracing these technological innovations thoughtfully, we can enhance our emotional skills and ultimately improve the quality of all our relationships. The digital age offers us unique opportunities for personal growth, but it's up to us to use them wisely, balancing tech use with offline experiences that also nurture our hearts and minds.

Leveraging Apps and Tools for Growth

In an era where technology is interwoven into the fabric of our daily lives, it offers not just a platform for communication but also an avenue for self-improvement and personal emotional development. More than just convenience, apps and digital tools can catalyze growth in emotional intelligence, providing opportunities to practice, understand, and refine our emotional capabilities in a digital context.

Imagine a world where an app on your phone isn't just a distraction, but a guide—a digital mentor that steers you toward better self-awareness and empathy. Today, such tools exist, designed intricately with algorithms that understand how you communicate, manage stress, and build connections. These apps can significantly enhance your emotional intelligence by offering insights and exercises tailored to your emotional needs. By leveraging data and artificial intelligence, they help identify patterns in your behavior, enabling you to see how your emotions fluctuate in various digital interactions.

Consider a tool that tracks your responses in emails or messages, offering a reflective view of your tone and sentiment. This isn't about surveillance; it's about self-discovery, helping you see patterns you might otherwise miss. Such feedback can be revelatory, allowing you to adjust your communication strategies to be more empathetic and considerate, fostering stronger, more trusting relationships in both personal and professional realms.

Beyond communication, digital tools can help in managing stress and emotional regulation, crucial for maintaining overall well-being in a fast-paced world. Mindfulness and meditation apps like Headspace or Calm provide guided sessions that can help you cultivate a practice of emotional regulation. These tools often come with features that can remind you to take breaks, breathe deeply, or engage in short meditations throughout your day, contributing to reduced stress and increased emotional control.

Even more interactive are apps designed for mental health and wellness, which offer virtual therapists powered by AI. These platforms not only provide coping strategies and mental exercises but also simulate conversations that help you process emotions, offering a safe space to unburden your mind. It's like having a therapist in your pocket, ready to guide you through moments of anxiety or emotional turmoil, empowering you to take charge of your emotional health.

Then there's the potential of gamifying emotional growth. Apps that incorporate game mechanics can make learning about emotional intelligence engaging and fun. By presenting users with scenarios that simulate real-life emotional challenges, these apps offer an interactive way to learn problem-solving, empathy, and conflict resolution. As you progress through levels, you sharpen these skills, receiving instant feedback that helps reinforce learning and encourage personal growth.

Still, it's essential to tread carefully in this digital landscape. Tools and apps are just that—tools. While they provide valuable support and insights, they are no substitute for genuine human interaction and the complexity of face-to-face communication. Balancing the use of digital tools with real-world emotional experiences is crucial for developing a holistic approach to emotional intelligence. Remember, these applications serve as supplements to your growth, not replacements.

Moreover, privacy concerns should not be overlooked. As these tools collect and analyze your data to personalize your experience, safeguarding your information is paramount. Always opt for apps that are transparent about their data use policies and prioritize your security. Your emotional journey is personal, and maintaining that intimacy and trust is a priority for sustainable growth.

On a broader scale, leveraging these digital tools can prepare us for the future of emotional intelligence, where technology will increasingly play a central role. As AI becomes more sophisticated, it will not only analyze but anticipate emotional states, offering support that's both proactive and preventive. The potential for these innovations is vast, promising to transform how we nurture our emotional selves in the digital age.

In conclusion, technology offers not just challenges but immense opportunities for growth in personal emotional development. By intelligently leveraging apps and tools, we can enhance our emotional intelligence, preparing ourselves for the complexities of digital interactions. It's about creating a digital toolkit that supports our journey toward becoming more emotionally aware and adept in both online and offline spaces. Let these technologies be your allies in the pursuit of emotional growth, guiding you toward a more empathetic, connected, and fulfilled life.

The Future of AI and Emotional Intelligence

The interplay between artificial intelligence and emotional intelligence presents one of the most intriguing frontiers in technology and personal development. As AI continues to evolve, it's not just about machines becoming smarter or more efficient; it's also about their potential to enrich our emotional lives and how we interact with them. This transformation isn't hypothetical or distant; it's unfolding right now, shifting the way we understand and harness our emotions and empathy in digital contexts.

The first step in this transformation is recognizing AI's capability in sensing and interpreting emotions. Today, AI systems can analyze text, speech, and even facial expressions to gauge emotional states. But what does this mean for personal emotional development? Imagine digital assistants that don't just remind us about meetings but also check in on our emotional well-being, offering support or suggesting activities to boost our mood. Such interactions are not just transactional but transformational, building a bridge between analytical data and emotional support.

Moreover, AI has the potential to personalize emotional intelligence training on an unprecedented scale. With AI's ability to process vast amounts of data, it can tailor emotional development programs to individual needs, learning styles, and emotional states. For instance, apps could adapt in real time to provide personalized feedback and exercises aimed at enhancing specific emotional intelligence components like empathy or self-regulation. This personalized approach ensures that emotional growth becomes an integral and continuous part of our daily lives, much like physical fitness.

However, alongside these possibilities, we must also consider the ethical implications. The capability of AI to understand and manipulate emotions brings with it questions about privacy and consent. How should data about our emotional states be collected, used, or shared? Users must remain at the center of this discussion, ensuring that AI-enhanced emotional tools empower rather than exploit. Transparent practices and informed consent should be non-negotiable aspects of this technological evolution.

In workplaces, AI's integration into emotional intelligence could reshape team dynamics. Virtual teams, increasingly common in our connected world, face challenges in communication that AI can help mitigate. Consider AI-driven platforms that gauge team sentiment, highlight communication gaps, or track emotional responses to group interactions. Such tools can lead to more cohesive, emotionally intelligent teams that navigate both achievements and challenges with greater awareness and empathy.

Moreover, AI holds the promise of democratizing emotional intelligence education. Traditionally, training in emotional skills required time, money, and access to specialized resources. With AI, these barriers can be dismantled. People from diverse backgrounds, regardless of their socioeconomic status, can access tailored emotional intelligence training, fostering a more empathetic and understanding society at large.

Looking at a larger scale, AI's integration with emotional intelligence could influence societal norms surrounding empathy and interaction. As AI systems begin to model empathetic listening or conflict resolution, they set benchmarks for desirable behavior in digital interactions. This modeling isn't about AI overtaking human interactions but enhancing them, providing examples of patience, understanding, and reflective listening that users can learn from and incorporate into their interactions, both online and offline.

Nonetheless, it's crucial to understand the boundaries of AI's emotional capabilities. While machines can simulate emotional understanding, they don't experience emotions as humans do. This distinction is important as we set realistic expectations for AI systems. Their role is to augment our emotional competencies, not to replace the uniquely human experiences of feeling and connecting. Our human consciousness and experience will always hold a depth that machines cannot replicate.

As AI continues to evolve within emotional intelligence landscapes, collaboration between technologists, psychologists, and ethicists will play a pivotal role in shaping ethical guidelines and best practices. Engaging diverse perspectives ensures that the technology addresses genuine human needs while avoiding pitfalls of bias and misapplication. A collaborative approach guarantees a balance between innovation and empathy, steering technology towards its most beneficial outcomes.

In sum, the future of AI intertwined with emotional intelligence promises significant advancements in personal and collective emotional development. As these developments unfold, they invite us to reconsider how we engage with both technology and each other. As AI becomes a partner in our emotional journeys, we must remain vigilant stewards of this integration, ensuring it promotes context-appropriate understanding, nurtures authentic connections, and nurtures personal growth.

The symbiosis of AI and emotional intelligence opens a new chapter in personal and interpersonal development. Embracing this fusion with an open, yet critical mind can lead to incredible strides in how we connect, learn, and grow emotionally in our digital world. As we look ahead, it's clear that rather than distant prospects, the future of AI and emotional intelligence is a pathway actively being carved today, inviting all of us to participate in its navigation.

Chapter 12: Lifelong Learning and Emotional Intelligence

In our ever-evolving digital era, the pursuit of knowledge never truly ends. Lifelong learning isn't just a commitment to expanding technical skills or updating professional know-how; it's a continuous evolution of our emotional intelligence. The pace of technological change demands that we not only adapt quickly but also understand the emotional intricacies that accompany such shifts. When we embrace lifelong learning, we also commit to enhancing our emotional intelligence to navigate this shifting landscape effectively.

Recognizing our own emotional responses to change is vital. As new technologies reshape our work and personal environments, we often encounter emotions such as anxiety, frustration, or even exhilaration. Identifying these feelings allows us to harness them constructively. Emotional intelligence teaches us to redirect these emotions, transforming potential negativity into opportunities for growth. It's about fostering a mindset that sees challenges as stepping stones rather than stumbling blocks.

But self-awareness is only the beginning. To cultivate a more profound emotional intelligence, we must also maintain an open dialogue with the world around us. Interpersonal relationships gain new dimensions as digital communication tools evolve. Continuously refining how we connect, empathize, and support others becomes an enriching part of our learning journey. By honing these skills, we deepen our understanding of emotional cues and nuances, both online and offline.

Strategies for continuous growth in emotional intelligence don't have to be complex. Simple practices like regular reflection, seeking feedback, and engaging in genuine conversations can profoundly impact our emotional dexterity. Mindful learning encourages us to ask ourselves: What can I learn from this experience? How can it boost my emotional repertoire? By approaching learning with curiosity and humility, we open ourselves to new possibilities.

Ultimately, lifelong learning intertwined with emotional intelligence empowers us to lead more fulfilling lives. As we grow emotionally, we're better equipped to face the uncertainties of a technologically driven world, forging stronger, more compassionate connections along the way.

Adapting Emotional Skills in a Changing World

In a world that's constantly evolving, our emotional skills need to keep pace with the changing dynamics. From the rise of virtual meetings to the way social media shapes our interactions, the landscape is vastly different from even a decade ago. Addressing these changes not only requires awareness but a proactive approach to cultivating emotional intelligence (EI) that's adaptable. This adaptability is not about discarding timeless emotional skills but refining and applying them across new mediums and contexts.

One significant aspect of adapting emotional skills is recognizing how digital platforms affect our interactions. Text messages, emails, video calls, and social media posts demand a new form of emotional literacy. You're often required to decode feelings with limited cues. Unlike face-to-face interactions, these platforms lack the full spectrum of human expression—tone of voice, facial expressions, and body language are often hard to interpret. Thus, the first task in adapting is honing your ability to read the subtext of digital communications while being mindful of your own emotional signals.

Adapting emotional skills is partly about self-awareness: understanding your emotional responses to digital environments. Are you more prone to irritation when emails are overly formal? Does seeing a flood of curated, picture-perfect lives on social media lead to feelings of inadequacy? Recognizing these triggers is crucial. Use your awareness as a springboard for growth, acknowledging how digital situations affect emotions differently than face-to-face ones.

Transitioning emotional skills into digital formats also involves empathy development. To be empathic online, you can't rely on traditional methods; you must develop a sensitivity to digital cues. A delayed response doesn't necessarily mean disinterest, and a brief message isn't inherently rude. Learning to give the benefit of the doubt helps cultivate empathy in these scenarios, filling the space where nonverbal cues are missing. It's about interpreting and responding with kindness and consideration.

The digital age also requires a reconsideration of emotional boundaries. Technology blurs lines between personal and professional spaces, demanding constant connectivity. This can lead to stress and burnout, making it vital to establish digital boundaries. Deciding when and how to engage, and carving out time for disconnecting, is essential. This not only protects your emotional well-being but also enhances your interactions when you are online, leading to more genuine and productive engagements.

As individuals, the task extends beyond personal adaptation. It's about influencing the broader environment where these interactions occur. By modeling strong emotional intelligence, you encourage others to engage thoughtfully. It's a ripple effect—a small shift in one person can influence an entire group. Whether you're part of a virtual team or engaging with a global community online, your approach can set the tone for meaningful connections.

Emotionally adapting in a changing world also ties into continuous learning. The tools, platforms, and ways we communicate today may not be the same tomorrow. Developing a mindset that embraces change and values emotional intelligence across new formats is paramount. This involves being open to new learning experiences, technological or emotional, and recognizing that learning never stops.

Furthermore, technology itself is an ally in cultivating emotional intelligence. There are apps and tools designed to assist in emotional regulation and empathy training. These can supplement traditional methods, offering interactive ways to practice and refine emotional skills. Embracing these tools with curiosity rather than skepticism can facilitate growth, providing new avenues for enhancing your emotional toolkit.

In essence, adapting emotional skills as the world changes requires a combination of self-reflection, empathy expansion, boundary setting, and continuous learning. It's about evolving alongside technology and using it to foster healthier, more authentic connections. By doing so, you not only enrich your personal and professional life but also contribute positively to the digital communities you're part of.

Ultimately, much of this journey involves letting go of the fear of digital transformation and looking at change as an opportunity for growth. In each challenge lies a chance to become more emotionally intelligent. By embracing these changes with open eyes and a committed heart, we can thrive emotionally in a digital world while maintaining the humanity that underpins all meaningful interactions.

Strategies for Continuous Growth

In this ever-evolving digital landscape, continuous growth is no longer just an option; it's essential. The world around us is changing at an unprecedented pace, and with these shifts, emotional intelligence must evolve too. The journey of lifelong learning will empower tech-savvy individuals to refine their emotional capabilities, paving the way for richer digital and face-to-face interactions. Let's delve into strategies for fostering this continuous growth, building on the critical foundation of emotional intelligence.

One effective strategy is to cultivate a mindset of curiosity and openness. Staying curious is about embracing the unknown and being eager to explore new perspectives. This mindset invites opportunities for learning and innovation, both vital components of emotional growth. When you're driven by curiosity, you're more likely to question assumptions, listen actively, and seek to understand, all of which enhance your emotional intelligence. By remaining open to new experiences and diverse viewpoints, you nurture empathy and emotional adaptability, essential qualities in today's interconnected world.

Engaging in reflective practices is another cornerstone for continuous growth. Self-reflection allows you to assess your own emotional responses and understand why you feel the way you do. Dedicate time each day or week to consider your interactions and emotional reactions—what went well, what could've been handled differently, and how your emotions have influenced your decisions. This reflective process leads to greater self-awareness and helps fine-tune your emotional responses in digital environments.

Setting SMART goals—goals that are Specific, Measurable, Achievable, Relevant, and Time-bound—can significantly aid in targeting and tracking your emotional growth. For instance, if you aim to improve your ability to manage stress in virtual meetings, a SMART goal might involve learning specific stress-reduction techniques, practicing them in controlled settings, and implementing them in real time. Tracking this progress over weeks or months ensures you stay focused and can adapt your strategies if needed.

Embrace lifelong learning by actively seeking educational opportunities that challenge and expand your emotional intelligence. Online courses, workshops, and seminars focused on emotional skills can provide valuable insights and techniques. These learning environments encourage interaction and discussion, enabling you to practice emotional skills in real-time and receive feedback. Explore diverse topics, from digital communication to leadership skills, each offering unique perspectives that enrich your emotional toolkit.

Building a support network of peers who value emotional intelligence is another powerful strategy. Surround yourself with individuals who challenge, support, and inspire your emotional development. These connections can offer feedback, share experiences, and provide accountability, pushing you toward continuous improvement. Peer groups or professional networks focused on emotional intelligence can be instrumental in maintaining motivation and discovering new growth paths.

Emotional resilience, the ability to adaptively respond to change and adversity, is crucial for ongoing growth. Life and work in a digital era often come with unexpected challenges. By developing resilience, you're better equipped to bounce back from setbacks and learn from experiences. Techniques like mindfulness meditation, journaling, or stress management exercises help cultivate resilience, allowing you to approach digital missteps as learning opportunities rather than failures.

Celebrate your milestones, no matter how small. Recognizing achievements in emotional growth reinforces positive behavior and fosters motivation to continue learning. It's easy to overlook progress, especially when it doesn't create immediate, tangible results. Take time to reflect on and appreciate how far you've come; it creates a sense of accomplishment and reignites the desire to face future challenges head-on.

Remember that growth in emotional intelligence is not linear. It involves setbacks and periods of rapid gain and is uniquely individual. Be patient and forgiving with yourself as you navigate this journey. Understand that emotional intelligence is a skill that can always be refined, and there's no final destination—only continuous evolution.

In an era where technology is pervasive and ever-evolving, your ability to adapt and grow emotionally is more vital than ever. Embrace these strategies for continuous growth, allowing them to be your compass as you navigate both digital and personal landscapes. By doing so, you empower yourself to foster more meaningful relationships online and offline, enhancing not only your own emotional well-being but also contributing positively to the emotional climate of those you interact with. Adopt a spirit of discovery and commitment to emotional learning—your future self will thank you for it.

Conclusion

In a world where pixels often replace face-to-face encounters, mastering emotional intelligence is no longer a luxury; it's essential. As we've journeyed through the chapters of this book, a compelling picture has emerged of how vital emotional intelligence is to bridging the digital divide between human beings. It's a transformative skill set that empowers us not just to cope but to thrive, enabling genuine connection in both virtual and physical realms.

The digital age presents both challenges and opportunities. On one hand, technology connects us with people across the globe, fostering diverse relationships and collaborative possibilities. On the other, it can create emotional distance, misunderstandings, and a sometimes overwhelming flood of information. Emotional intelligence becomes our compass, guiding us to meaningful interactions and helping us maintain our emotional equilibrium.

Our exploration began with defining emotional intelligence in the context of today's digital landscape, emphasizing its evolving nature. We delved into the core components that constitute EI, recognizing their relevance in both online and offline interactions. Understanding these foundational aspects allows us to intentionally apply them in digital communications, elevating our ability to navigate diverse dialogues and forge deeper connections.

Empathy in particular plays a transformative role in digital interactions. The screens that separate us should not be barriers but windows into understanding others' perspectives and emotions. By honing our ability to read online emotional cues, we're better equipped to respond with compassion and authenticity. This fosters trust and strengthens relationships, reinforcing the human aspect in a world increasingly mediated by technology.

Digital self-awareness serves as another cornerstone in developing emotional intelligence. Being mindful of our online presence and recognizing our emotional triggers enable us to manage how we present ourselves and react in digital spaces. This self-regulation not only enhances our interactions but also nurtures our inner emotional well-being.

The digital realm offers ample opportunities but also necessitates the establishment of healthy boundaries. To balance connectivity with emotional well-being, it's crucial to craft spaces both online and offline where we can recharge and process our experiences. Prioritizing offline emotional fulfillment ensures that our digital engagements are enriching rather than depleting.

These skills take on even greater importance in professional settings, particularly with the rise of remote work and virtual teams. Emotional intelligence enhances team dynamics, osters strong leadership, and helps navigate the unique challenges of leading from a distance. By integrating emotional skills into digital leadership, we cultivate environments where creativity, productivity, and personal growth flourish.

Social media, too, demands a conscious application of emotional intelligence. The ability to manage emotional responses on these platforms protects our mental health and preserves our authenticity. By remaining true to ourselves and how we interact online, we can use these spaces as powerful tools for connection and self-expression.

Looking to the future, technology will continue to play a significant role in our personal emotional development. Emerging tools and apps offer innovative ways to enhance our emotional intelligence, while AI is poised to provide new dimensions of support and learning. Embracing these advancements with an open yet critical mindset will enable us to unlock new potentials in emotional intelligence.

In sum, lifelong learning is an integral part of our emotional intelligence journey. As the world around us changes, so too must our skills and strategies evolve. Adaptability and continuous growth in emotional intelligence will empower us to navigate the complexities of modern life with resilience and empathy.

Ultimately, harnessing emotional intelligence in the digital age is about creating and maintaining authentic, meaningful connections in every facet of our lives. It serves as the bridge between technology and humanity, enabling us to find common ground and nurture relationships whether we're tapping on keyboards or speaking face-to-face. With these insights and tools in hand, the power to transform our interactions and enrich our lives is distinctly within our reach.

Appendix A: Appendix

The journey through understanding and applying emotional intelligence in our digital lives is profound and multifaceted. This appendix serves as a supporting resource, providing additional insights and references to help you further explore the concepts discussed throughout the book. Whether you're seeking to deepen your knowledge or find practical tools for daily application, this section aims to guide and inspire your continued growth.

Additional Resources

For those wanting to explore more about emotional intelligence, especially in the context of the digital world, consider the following resources:

- **Books:** There are numerous books that delve into emotional intelligence, offering diverse perspectives and strategies. Look for works from authors who specialize in psychology and digital communication to enhance your understanding.

- **Online Courses:** Platforms like Coursera, edX, and LinkedIn Learning offer courses on emotional intelligence. These can provide structured learning paths and interactive components to reinforce your skills.

- **Workshops and Webinars:** Explore interactive workshops and webinars that focus on emotional intelligence in digital settings. They often provide real-time interaction, enhancing your ability to apply the skills in practical scenarios.

Tools for Practice

Incorporating emotional intelligence into your daily digital interactions can be achieved with the help of various tools and techniques:

- **Mindfulness Apps:** Apps like Headspace and Calm can help you practice mindfulness, a key component of emotional self-regulation. Regular use can improve your ability to manage emotions online.

- **Journaling Platforms:** Digital journaling tools like Day One or Journey encourage self-reflection, allowing you to monitor and understand your emotional triggers within digital interactions.

- **Communication Enhancers:** Utilizing platforms that focus on improving communication skills, such as Grammarly or non-verbal cue training apps, can enhance how you express yourself across digital platforms.

Further Study and Exploration

Learning is an ongoing process. As you continue to cultivate emotional intelligence, consider engaging in communities and networks that emphasize these skills:

- **Forums and Discussion Groups:** Platforms like Reddit or specialized forums offer spaces to exchange experiences and insights with others focused on emotional intelligence in digital scenarios.

- **Podcasts and Videos:** Access content that provides interviews with experts and real-life applications of emotional intelligence, further expanding your understanding and perspective.

In a world that's constantly evolving, embracing the journey of enhancing emotional intelligence in digital interactions is not just beneficial, it's essential. By using these resources and tools, you're well-equipped to continue growing and thriving both online and offline.

www.ingramcontent.com/pod-product-compliance
Lightning Source LLC
Chambersburg PA
CBHW070124230526
45472CB00004B/1403